Praise for *School for the Age of Upheaval*

"*School for the Age of Upheaval* brings to jagged relief the struggles of American adolescents in this time of anxiety and inequity. With unique and powerful prose, T. Elijah Hawkes stirs us with the stories, poetry, and voices of his yearning and despairing students. Fortunately, Hawkes also provides us with key insights from his experience as an educational leader from which city schools and rural communities can draw to successfully support, teach, and heal our teenagers as they transition from childhood to adulthood."
—Shael Polakow-Suransky, president, Bank Street College of Education

"Clear-eyed and visionary, *School for the Age of Upheaval* is a powerful call to action and reflection. If schools are where the next generation is either crushed or comes alive, this book is a vivifying force. Hawkes is unflinching in his diagnosis of the pain and violence enacted by and on our youth and stubbornly hopeful and pragmatic about what we can do about it. He pours over twenty years of experience from New York City to rural Vermont into these pages, foregrounding the experiences of teens whose personal upheavals intersect with the social upheavals that are confronting us all. *School for the Age of Upheaval* maps a way forward that is pragmatic and bold, a courageous curriculum that does not deny or pacify the anger and disillusionment expressed by young people but acknowledges and channels it into a positive force. Beautifully written and passionately argued, this is a book that every teacher, administrator, public official, and parent should read—not once, but as an ongoing tool to help realign everyday practices in our schools with a broader vision of education as a site of social transformation."
—Ruha Benjamin, Princeton University, and author, *Race after Technology*

"Politically conscious educators are deeply motivated to develop the leadership of young people with the hopes of building a more just democracy—and yet, like all educators, they are so often demoralized and devalued in their work. *School for the Age of Upheaval* is an offering to sustain their teaching and celebrate their contributions. T. Elijah Hawkes subverts deficit-model thinking by laying out how youth are developing new strategies for digesting what they're presented with—whether messages of religion, the street, or social media. Young people are not passive victims, and we can find hope in the evidence and thoughtful analysis in this book. Adults can find it difficult to comprehend what today's children and young people are going through. It can feel like too much for our hearts and minds when we consider what today's youth have to process, filter, and absorb, but Hawkes tells these stories so that our hearts and minds are fed while we consider the real and figurative sea change we're living through."—Sally Lee, founder and executive director, Teachers Unite

"It isn't a superficial 'strategy' that T. Elijah Hawkes is offering us—a useful strategy for handling 'those' kids. This book reminds us that what we need is authentic respect and love. It's all about trust. Hawkes beautifully narrates what it takes to build trust as the foundation for courageous teaching."
—Deborah Meier, former senior scholar at New York University's Steinhardt School of Education; MacArthur Award–winning founder of the Central Park East Schools in New York and the Mission Hill School in Boston; author of *The Power of Their Ideas: Lessons for America from a Small School in Harlem* and *In Schools We Trust*; and cofounder of the Coalition of Essential Schools

"*School for the Age of Upheaval* provides vitally important, frontline-deep insight into the anger, depression, anxiety, violence, and pain of America's youth. That insight is beautifully framed by a caring, experienced, and uniquely urban and rural leading American educator. Teachers will immediately recognize the truth in the raw reality of the trauma and search for meaning and power our students communicate every day. Non-educators get a genuine under-the-hood explanation of all that American adolescent confusion, posturing, and pain, paired with direction on what can and should be done about it. This book reaches into the abyss of shallow culture and broken communities to provide a frontline explanation of the pain and posturing that our American rural and urban youth are expressing as they attempt to find authenticity, meaning, and something real to hold onto."—Mike McRaith, Vermont Principals Association

"With an eye trained especially on troubled adolescents, T. Elijah Hawkes writes movingly of a generation denied 'a mature cultural inheritance' and proposes a schooling that can heal the wounds and open new possibilities for a more compelling education and a healthier society. This is a must-read not just for teachers but for all who seek a new, more progressive direction in education."—B. Edward McClellan, professor emeritus, Indiana University, and author of *Moral Education in America*

"If you are concerned about the practice and the prospect of democratic education, then you must read T. Elijah Hawkes. Hawkes makes that duty a great pleasure with an elegant, erudite prose style that deftly applies years of teaching and administrative experience to the vexing problems of public education. Hawkes demonstrates the power of compassionate understanding and rigorous maturity in narratives of school life. His evocations of daily life in public school provide rich insights into the experience of teaching and learning. Hawkes has the compassion to see each child as an individual, he has the courage to understand the implications of each event for his own work as a school leader, and he has the wisdom born of many years of reading and study to describe the path from current problems and failures to the future health of democratic education."—Andy Kaplan, editor, *Schools: Studies in Education*

"T. Elijah Hawkes is a gifted writer and a powerful storyteller. He is also one of the most radical thinkers in the United States. Why? Saying that teachers and students should be empowered—this is something we have heard for decades because it is only rarely done. The implications of such empowerment are not lost on those who prefer the status quo. *School for the Age of Upheaval* provides the theoretical framework and the practical tools to empower a school and transform a society."—John Samuel Tieman, PhD, cochair, Schools Committee, American Psychoanalytic Association

School for the Age of Upheaval

School for the Age of Upheaval

*Classrooms That Get Personal,
Get Political, and
Get to Work*

T. Elijah Hawkes

ROWMAN & LITTLEFIELD
Lanham • Boulder • New York • London

Published by Rowman & Littlefield
An imprint of The Rowman & Littlefield Publishing Group, Inc.
4501 Forbes Boulevard, Suite 200, Lanham, Maryland 20706
www.rowman.com

6 Tinworth Street, London SE11 5AL, United Kingdom

British Library Cataloguing in Publication Information Available

Library of Congress Cataloging-in-Publication Data Available

ISBN 978-1-4758-5181-6 (cloth)
ISBN 978-1-4758-5182-3 (pbk.)
ISBN 978-1-4758-5183-0 (ebook)

Only a lot of boys and girls?
Only the tiresome spelling, writing, ciphering classes?
Only a Public School?

Ah more, infinitely more; . . .

And you, America,
Cast you the real reckoning for your present?
The lights and shadows of your future—good or evil?
To girlhood, boyhood look—the Teacher and the School.
                         —Walt Whitman, "An Old Man's Thought of School"

Ninety percent of adolescents in the area were left with PTSD, with the
average adolescent boy registering in the high end of the range of "severe" PTSD, and the average teenage girl registering over the threshold of
"very severe." Six months after the storm, four out of every five teenage
survivors from Posoltega suffered from depression; more than half, the
study found, compulsively nursed what the authors called, a bit euphe-
mistically, "vengeful thoughts."
    —David Wallace-Wells, on the impact of Hurricane Mitch on children in
                              Nicaragua, *The Uninhabitable Earth*

A riot is the language of the unheard.
                         —Martin Luther King Jr., "The Other America"

Contents

Preface

Screen or Shovel?

When my son was five years old, we were home together on a summer Saturday. He wanted to stay inside. It wasn't the time of day we allowed him to watch television, but he was asking. There was a small tantrum when I refused, telling him he had to come outside with me instead to work in the yard.

The past week, we had dug up some broken bricks that formed a small patio in front of the house, and I'd decided that we were going to replace the bricks with dirt and seed with grass. We would get the dirt from a pile on the other side of the yard. I told him what we were going to do and that I wanted his help. He questioned why we were doing this and that. I explained. The bricks had been old and unstable, the holes where they'd once been now needed filling to be safe for walking, and the grass would look nice. He grumbled and came along.

He had a shovel very much like my shovel—a wooden shaft and a (smaller) metal blade. I grabbed my shovel and he grabbed his. I got the wheelbarrow. He got in for a fun little ride over to the dirt pile. We got to work.

For an hour we dug up dirt and brought it across the yard, back and forth. He found roles he was good at: tossing dirt with his shovel, picking out rocks and some weeds, stomping on the dirt to flatten it. At some point he paused in his efforts to tell me, "Daddy, last night, when I was going to bed, I was thinking about what I wanted to do today." I said, "Yeah, what were you thinking?" He said, "I was thinking that this was exactly what I wanted to do today."

Now, in reality, there's absolutely no way he could have had thought that. We had not discussed this phase of the project yet, and I'd not told him he'd be involved. But most children—from their younger years through adolescence—have a deep need to do work alongside important adults in their world. They have a need to feel competent executing appropriately scaffolded tasks with tools fitting their strength and skills. They have a need to do work that needs doing in the places where they live.

My son's more immediate interest that morning was to chew watermelon-flavored gum and watch a cartoon. His deeper developmental and emotional needs were quite different, however. So different, in fact, that he re-imagined his hopes and desires: he created a story about what he thought he wanted to do the night before so that it corresponded to the work he was doing with me.

This book is for educators who are interested in defining learning tasks for young people that correspond to their deeper developmental needs, as well as the social, economic, political, and cultural needs of their home and community. If schools can redefine relevance in this way, we will then find ourselves prioritizing and supporting work with political and ethical implications—and we'll find ourselves better supporting the needs and hopes of our children and our society.

Acknowledgments

For their comradeship and mentorship, I am grateful to educators at Humanities Preparatory Academy, the James Baldwin School, and Randolph Union High School. I am also grateful to the students who shared their stories with me and allowed them to be shared here. To my family, thank you for supporting me in this work. I love you. To the editors with whom I've collaborated over the years, thank you for the critique, encouragement, and opportunity to share my thoughts with others.

Introduction

A Time of Upheaval

Storms of my grandchildren—when will these hit with full force?
—James Hansen, *Storms of My Grandchildren*

Adolescence is a time of upheaval, a period rich with identity challenges, developmental changes, and revolutionary energy. This is true of young people growing up in any age or story. Cain and Abel were troubled boys. Icarus, too, who flew too close to the sun. Joan of Arc trampled convention, leading armies in her teens. Carlotta Walls LaNier was fourteen when she walked through the fire of bigotry to integrate Little Rock's Central High. Adolescent courage, angst, and daring are nothing new.

But to be an adolescent in a time like ours, when the broader society is experiencing great turbulence, presents special challenges to young people. It also presents special challenges to the communities educating these young people, communities that need them to grow up healthy, strong, and kind. There are risks if we don't rise to meet these challenges. It is dangerous when the potency of adolescence is channeled in the wrong directions.

STORM

In 2009, renowned climate scientist James Hansen wrote about "storms of my grandchildren," painting a sobering picture of storms to come. These storms and upheavals have arrived, and will continue to arrive, and with increasing force. These are the storms of my children: my two sons at home and the children I know as students at school. They are the droughts of this summer, the floods of last spring, the fires in California, the winds that crushed Puerto Rico. They are the Pentagon's threat multipliers, helping to shape new cradles of extremism and of war. They are grim reapers with gentle names like Harvey, Ida, Irene, Sandy, Ike, and Katrina. They are the angry cousins of much more mundane disruptions: the ticks new to my cousin's yard, the ash in my friend's Los Angeles pool, the soccer game cancelled because it's too hot.

And dreadful weather is but one element of the perfect storm gathering around children today. Environmental disturbance, economic segregation, enduring structural racism, authoritarian leaders with fascist leanings, public officials dedicated to dismantling the public sphere—when a generation is dealt a hand like this, it bodes darkly.

Not only could our world see storms that toss boulders the size of houses from the sea—Hansen's more recent warning[1]—hard times bring a willingness in many to toss aside the humanity of others. When we are afraid, we want freedom from fear, and too often we seek that freedom by putting ourselves in armor and others in chains.

But this is not a book about climate science or political science. This is a book about the troubles of adolescence in an increasingly troubled world, and how schools can help these children grow up to be compassionate and courageous citizens in communities that desperately need them to be so. The writings of young people will provide the point of departure. To respect confidentiality, in the stories I tell about schools, certain circumstances have been changed and all the names of students and adults are pseudonyms.

COMMUNITY CRUMBLING DOWN

Demographers and economists in recent years have been startled by a new trend: many white kids in the United States are growing up in communities where life expectancy is going down. The adults are dying earlier than before—by suicide, drug overdose, and by poisons that kill more slowly, like alcoholism.[2] This kind of trouble in the home can make for trouble in the hearts of children.

When adults struggle to meet their own basic needs, they will often struggle to meet the needs of their kids. Many parents are working two or more jobs and are not able to be present with their sons and daughters. Other parents are confined in jail or in the solitary service of an addiction. Some parents die too soon. And children, who are naturally self-centered and still limited in their understanding of cause and effect, will often translate this absence or abandonment as something for which they are to blame.

Directly or indirectly, when parents struggle, are absent, or die, children can see themselves as being at fault—as being faulty, bad, less worthy, worthless. And they will communicate their pain and punish themselves in various ways: with poor choices, with high-risk behaviors, with razors.

In chapter 1, we hear from girls in a rural and mostly white school community who are growing up in an adult world that seems to be crumbling down. The troubles in their families, the insecurities of adolescence, and the easy amplification of shame on social media conspire to make their lives painful. The younger girls don't do heroin to kill the pain—not yet. Before they try opiates to silence the pain, they first need to voice it, to have it felt and seen.

BEEN IN THE STORM SO LONG

Many of my fellow Americans would remind me—a white man with Pilgrim heritage and a painting in his home of a Maryland plantation, passed down for generations—that trouble like this is hardly new. It may feel new in some white communities, but to worry about a child born into a world that would destroy it, this is not a new worry for many. "Been in the storm so long," goes the song, "been in the storm so long, children."

Black lives matter to this book. In chapter 2, we listen to fifteen-year-old Jeremiah, and we consider the challenges of growing up in what Cornel West has called nihilist America, where violence abounds and community erodes.

Jeremiah briefly attended a New York City school for transfer students, youth who were looking for a second, sometimes third or fourth, chance at graduation. Like many schools in this country, it was a small, community-minded place where adults and young people got to know each other well. Jeremiah was only with them a short time, but he trusted the adults enough to share his writing: pages upon pages of rhymes, poems, letters, business plans, and other dreams. A journal, a songbook, a ledger. We will hear love in it, and the need for love. We will hear brute violence in his writing too. We adults may want to distance ourselves from it, but if we listen closely we will hear echoes of the dominant culture, refrains from our nation's own adult exhibitions of impulsivity, pleasure-seeking, and violent flights from vulnerability.

Our forty-fifth president was elected in part because of his willingness to speak like Jeremiah: enemies are conjured and destroyed, women are shamed and taken, wealth is confused with worth. In a world that rewards this worldview, when the dominant society models domination unashamed, when adult leaders tweet like tweens, when pain-killing and pleasure-seeking are ends unto themselves—where does this leave our adolescents?

It is important that many of us see something of ourselves—and the values of our broader society—in Jeremiah's unfiltered extremes:

Light up a blunt
Shoot and run
Not me
I put a couple more holes in him

Dull the pain, destroy the enemy, walk with swagger. These are the tropes of our mainstream culture; Jeremiah simply speaks in more raw verses. "Bleeding dead meat," he calls the body of the person he kills in his song, "put him down in the street." Fantasy or true story, adolescence is a time of extremism such as this. Frequent are the fantasies and full is the capacity for self-harm and harm to others, including the willingness to kill and be killed.

BIBLE AND BULLET

Unlike Jeremiah, who found much of his identity in the certainty of violence, a very different boy walked into a New York City school one day with a bullet. In chapter 3 we meet Roberto, a mild-mannered, tall, strong, gentle Hispanic boy who'd been beaten up in public during lunch after trying to be cordial to another guy's girlfriend.

Far from street-smart or street-nurtured, Roberto had no codes of battle to guide him in the wake of his humiliation. He had no idea what to do with his shame and rage. One day he brought a bullet to school and gave it to a teacher. Why? Did he also have a gun? In the days that followed, he couldn't—or wouldn't—explain the meaning of the bullet or his intentions. The school made him write about it.

"It was a calm night," he begins, "breeze felt good breathing on one's face." He recounts a dream in which a girl tells him that she herself had dreamt of his death, a mutilation by chainsaw. In written dialogue with his principal, Roberto pens several chapters. His story paints confusion. Far from a nihilist absence of meaning, in Roberto's swirling identity struggle he's in trouble because there's too much meaning, too many competing narratives: from religious traditions to Hollywood films, from cold hard street codes to the warmth of family, from bullets with hollow points to Bible verses.

We will read Roberto's stories, and will want him to find a way out of the confusion. We will wonder what powerful objects and identity stories young people can seize today to ground them. What path can they walk to get clarity at a time of terrific and terrifying identify confusion?

It is crucial that young people find some coherence and simplification. But there is danger in simplification, too. Oversimplified thinking can lead to ignorance and the dehumanization of others. It also brings violence, sometimes in terrorist extremes.

LEARNING FROM CRISIS

In chapter 4, we further consider the extremes of adolescence and what these can teach us. Two boys in a small New England town are alleged to have a plan to kill their classmates. Law enforcement intervenes, the boys are detained, and the school community is plunged into crisis. What can educators learn from such a crisis? What can we learn from homicidal or maybe-homicidal teens and their needs? What can they teach us about what all kids need?

The two boys were removed from their families and the community. Talk of the "kill list" was whispered in school hallways and about town. The school faculty wrestled with a sense of failure and surprise. For guidance, the principal reached out to an expert in homicide, schools, and adolescence. He helped the school reflect on how aggression can be channeled in ways that do not lead to violence.

Other thinkers, like psychologist Erik Erikson, can also help guide us in times of adolescent crisis. Erikson's reflections on identity development are important today, especially because of the similarities between the era in which he worked and the era we live in now. Erikson was concerned with identity development in Western civilization in an era marked by extraordinarily rapid changes in technology and social organization. He was concerned about kids growing up in a world troubled by population dislocation, white supremacy, and war.

More than a few parallels are being drawn today between the rise of fascism before World War II and the fascist DNA found in the body politic thriving in our time. Anti-democratic politicians are in ascendance, or have ascended. Institutional norms of dialogue and cooperation are breaking down. Intolerance of difference is gaining new voice and strength.

What do young people in such a world need from their school communities? How can we channel adolescent pain, questions, and aggression in directions that do not lead to violent or final solutions? Where are the dangers and the opportunities? How can educators uphold our most sacred duties to both care for our children and safeguard our democracy? We must ask these questions—and we must confront our doubts. Sometimes we may even wonder: *Can teachers and schools even make a difference?*

For all the troubling doubts, my own work as an educator in public schools gives me energy and hope. Hitler Youth had teachers. Schools played a role in the rise of Nazism. In other words: educators matter very much. We need to matter *in the right direction*. The second part of this book is about how to move our teaching and learning in that direction.

COURAGEOUS CURRICULUM

Calibrating school to meet the identity needs of youth, as well as the needs of the broader democratic society, involves both extracurricular efforts and careful work with the curriculum of the school day.

Traditional extracurricular elements of school can be effective in channeling adolescent aggression in productive directions. This happens through healthy athletic teams, after-school clubs, service-learning opportunities, good counseling, and meaningful rites of passage. Humane disciplinary interventions, such as restorative justice practices, are likewise essential. But extracurricular efforts will only reach so many students. And to call these activities extracurricular is not to diminish their importance, but to distinguish them from the teaching and learning that happens in the classroom, during the day, when all kids are present, and when teachers are there explicitly to work with and reach all students.

What my twenty years working with teens has taught me is that a typical day of classes needs to offer students more than abstract academic activities and a handful of cordial relationships. We need to open up the very content of the classroom to the emotional life of the whole child. Curriculum that is calibrated to meet the identity needs of adolescents and the broader society should organize itself around four imperatives:

- Invite and model the exploration of inner life
- Foment ideological dissonance and commitment
- Nourish self-awareness and self-control
- Cultivate dexterity in using adult tools to approach adult tasks

In other words, this is teaching and learning that's willing to *get personal*, *get political*, *get meta*, and *get to work*. The second part of this book is about how to cultivate teaching and learning of this sort, which is an essential means of cutting adolescent rage off at the pass and turning it down another path, before it turns to violence.

WE NEED THEIR ANGER

The violence our children are willing to do to themselves and others is a problem. But the root problem is the violence we do to them, the trouble that the world we've made will continue to visit upon them in years to come. The traumas of poverty, the degradation and sexual violence done to the female body, the derision heaped on difference by the dominant culture, the dislocations that come from environmental upheavals—all of these damage our children. And the rage they feel is born of that damage, the pain and the injustice of it.

I hear my former colleague, Rosa. As she watched the live feed of her black and brown brothers and sisters shutting down an interstate in Charlotte, North Carolina, Rosa tweeted from Oakland in 2016: "So much grief. We hurtin. There's a riot, asleep or awake, in all of us. We cope with injustice and trauma, until it becomes too heavy."[3]

For all of our efforts to kill it, pain will not be killed. It will become too heavy and then find outlet. But if the only outlet our youth can find is riots, terrorism, beat-downs, and suicide, then our world is in even deeper trouble. Our nation's response to the pain of youth mustn't only be pills and distraction. We need their anger, and we need it to find its voice.

Our best hope is that young people's pain and sense of injustice join in creative destruction: collaborative work that dismantles what's wrong and builds something new and better. Our schools are a place where this hope and work must live. If school communities don't take on this charge, and take it on with explicit allegiance to democracy and the common good, others will surely find ways to channel the industry, idealism, and aggression of youth in much more grim directions.

Part I

Only a Lot of Boys and Girls?

But let us return to that atmosphere of violence, that violence which is just under the skin.

—Franz Fanon, *The Wretched of the Earth*
(New York: Grove Weidenfeld, 1991), 71.

Chapter One

CUT

Percent of students who purposefully hurt themselves without wanting to die, past 12 months . . .
Percent of students who felt sad or hopeless for two weeks in a row, past 12 months . . .
Percent of students who made a suicide plan, past 12 months . . .
—Vermont Youth Risk Behavior Survey, Items 1.09, 1.10, 1.11[1]

Pain carried inside will find outlet, and cutting one's own skin is one way to let it out. Self-harm is self-expression, and tells a story that simultaneously confirms the pain and distracts from the deeper hurt. In a society that dishes out trouble to kids in relentless fashion, educators and other adults who work with children have a choice: We can ask to hear their voices, invite and value their stories, or we can watch them write their stories in their scars.

The e-mail came out of nowhere in the middle of summer. It said, "Jenny Jeffries has invited you to edit the following document: *going down*." It was the summer between Jenny's seventh and eighth grade year, and she was sending Paula an invitation to a Google Doc. Paula was Jenny's middle school counselor. She'd once heard Jenny read her poems when visiting a creative writing class Jenny had taken in seventh grade. When they passed in the hallway later that day, Paula told Jenny that she'd love to hear more of her poetry sometime. Jenny smiled.

The school year ended, a month passed, and then, in the quiet middle of summer, Jenny sent Paula a link to the document in which she'd compiled many of her poems. The first of these was "My demons":

My pain flows through me like the blood that floods out of my smooth skin,
Or a rapid river flowing into a desperate sea.
My heart skips beats when you look into my eyes.

3

I stopped checking under my bed for the monsters,
I found that the only monster I fear is myself.

All I think about is how you told me I was beautiful
And how your warmth felt when you held me in your arms.

I closed my eyes and opened my wounds.
In the end, how can I run from what's inside of me?
I have so much to say,
But I can't seem to find the words.
5 out of 10 of the voices in my head tell me to pull the trigger.

Concerned about how urgent some of the sentiments might be, Paula responded immediately to ask Jenny when this, the most pain-laden poem in the collection, had been written. Paula wrote, "This is a beautiful, powerful couplet, Jenny: 'I closed my eyes and opened my wounds. In the end, how can I run from what's inside of me.' When did you write this poem?"

Jenny responded that same day, "I wrote the first at the end of last school year when I was going through one of the most life-challenging events I've ever gone through. That is what inspired me."

Paula was relieved, for she knew Jenny had received supports to help her through that difficult time. Paula planned to stay in touch over the summer, and told Jenny she looked forward to seeing her in the fall. She also said she looked forward to reading more of her poetry.

Summer passed, and Jenny walked into Paula's office the second day of school to ask if they could talk. She seemed ill at ease. Paula asked a few questions and listened. Jenny was insightful in describing what was unsettling her. She spoke of the new teachers she didn't yet know or trust, and said she was feeling sensitive to the behavior of status-seeking peers. Also, she was feeling low, having not taken her medication that day.

The second day of school happened to be a Friday, and this concerned Paula. The weekend can be isolating and difficult for students sometimes. Paula asked Jenny if she'd missed her meds on purpose, or if it was an accident. Jenny said it was an accident. Paula believed her, but knowing about the past lows in her emotional health, she told Jenny she wanted her to check in again before leaving for the weekend. Jenny agreed. Then they talked about her poems.

Jenny said she wished her peers took her poetry as seriously as she did. Paula suggested she could help the school form a poetry club, and Jenny lit up at the idea. Paula told her she would e-mail two faculty members who might like to be advisors to such a club. After she went to class, Paula called Jenny's last-period teacher and asked that she be sent down to see her briefly before the final bell.

"HOW CAN I RUN FROM WHAT'S INSIDE OF ME?"

The blood "floods out." Perhaps with a blade or tip that cuts or pierces, she lets the blood out. The blood runs out of her skin, but she cannot run from the blood; she asks, "how can I run from what's inside of me?" She can't. It is visible, not to be denied. There is certainty in it, an outer confirmation of her inner pain.

Is this what cutting does? Provide certainty? *My pain is real. I am real. I exist.* Or is it the adrenalin? The way the rush of endorphins at the surface allows a brief overwhelming of the deeper pain below? Or is it a punishment of the body belonging to a child who believes she deserves punishing, who believes she's bad because the world has treated her badly?

The writings of young people can help answer these questions. *My Secret Addiction: Teens Write about Cutting* is the title of a book of essays by young people writing for Youth Communication, a nonprofit youth-centered publisher in New York City. The writers offer us some understanding of why young people engage in self-harm. A writer who goes by the name Christa G. writes in the book's opening essay:

> I first cut myself when I was 13. I was feeling depressed and dead inside. I noticed a box of blades lying on the kitchen shelf. I took a blade and carried it to my room.
> I closed the door, mulled it over for about a minute, and then made a small vertical cut, about a centimeter long, to the underside of my left wrist. At first I felt nothing, as usual, and then came the pain—like a paper cut—and the feeling that a door had been opened. My heart beat really fast and I felt a rush; I felt powerful, and alive.[2]

Cutting helped this young person open a door. She didn't feel "dead" anymore. She felt herself, "powerful and alive."

In addition to meeting the self's need to confirm itself as powerful and real, cutting is also a form of communication to the outer world. A writer who calls herself Christine M. writes in the book's next essay about a therapist who helped her understand "why I do it." She writes:

> I started to understand that I really do have feelings, many feelings. As a child, I felt so much shame, anger and pain about the abuse I endured that I didn't know how to express it, and no one helped me talk about it. So I tried to bury those feelings, but also to communicate them through hurting myself.[3]

Christine M. felt bad about herself, and she communicated this by treating her body badly. Her confessions resonate with what professionals say about why children cut. "Cutting," writes psychoanalyst Mary Brady, "can represent both an attack on an object and/or an identification with an abused object." Cutting is the abuse of a body the world has signaled is worthy of abuse. Brady remarks how this concept can be useful to therapists who might struggle "to treat patients who both inflict cruelty on themselves and also suffer the cruelty."[4]

It is a useful idea for educators, too, who might work with children who cut and who might rightly wonder why a child would join forces with agents of brutality in her world by treating herself brutally. Teachers and others predisposed to see the goodness and great potential in a child can understand-ably be confused by the beautiful and talented girl who seems to devalue herself by cutting her own body.

Parallel confusion can reside in the mind of the child. One friend says you look good in that outfit, and the next girl says you dress like a slut. A boy at the dance says you're the one, and the next day he discards you. Teachers and counselors say you're smart, you can do it, you can do anything you set your mind to. Then a voice in the hall or an instant message asks why you haven't killed yourself yet. The child will wonder: *Who is right? Who am I? Am I worthy of this abuse, or not?*

THE CUTTING VOICE

Big identity questions don't like to go unanswered for long. For many young people, cutting ends the questions—for a time—allowing identification of and with the abused object or self. Visible punishment of the body provides outward and tangible objectification of inner pain.

Psychologist Ernest Becker wrote about this topic in his Pulitzer Prize–winning meditation on mortality, *The Denial of Death*. He is con-cerned with how people—children and adults—tame the terror felt when confronting powerful and hostile forces that can make them feel vulnerable, afraid, and alone. Feeling small and weak, we seek, says Becker, some de-gree of control.

Sometimes it is the body—even in illness or pain—that becomes the "object" a person can most effectively control. "The pains we feel," he writes, "the illnesses that are real or imaginary give us something to relate to, to keep us from slipping out of the world, from bogging down in the despera-tion of complete loneliness and emptiness." In the absence of more positive ways to find a sense of self and power in an overwhelming world, illness and pain can at least make us "feel real" and give us "a little purchase on our fate."[5]

Sometimes these feelings of being "real" are attained very privately: the person who cuts her skin and hides the cutting. This person is talking to herself, about herself. But even in this, the cutting is communication, and sooner or later the child will share it with someone.

"The symptom of self-cutting in adolescence is a communication that needs to 'cut through the silence' and to be heard by another," writes Mary Brady. "A hyperbolic expression that a containing skin has failed, cutting is the adolescent shouting this failure through his or her body. If the shout is not heard then the adolescent may have to escalate into increasingly self-destructive acts."[6]

One intention in breaking the skin is to break a silence, to shock an ignorant or ignoring world into response. And the adults in the child's world must respond. Peers can play an important role here too. Friends may well know of a young person's cutting before parents or other adults do.

In the school where Paula knew Jenny in her middle school years, there once was a high school girl in an art class with a substitute teacher, where things got a little bit rowdy. Students were moving too quickly around the room, putting supplies away, when an electric pencil sharpener got bumped, fell to the floor, and broke into pieces. Most of the pieces were plastic, but there were two small metal blades among the dusty pencil shavings. The student knelt and secretly took the blades. She then took the hand of a friend and took her to the bathroom. She gave her friend a blade. She cut her own skin. She invited her friend. But her friend didn't take the blade. Perhaps she didn't have the same story to tell—or not in that way. Instead, after leaving the bathroom, her friend went and told a school counselor. A response from adults followed, and an effective intervention.

Brady emphasizes the importance of responding to early self-cutting, before such behaviors evolve into entrenched habits. If the cutting can be heard, "it can become possible for the adolescent to begin to connect to a symbolic narrative rather than being tied to physical expressions."[7] It is the role of those of us who see/hear the cutting voice to help turn that narrative from one written in cuts to one written in other symbols.

"YOU'RE IN THIS HOLE"

At rates significantly higher than the state average, the girls in Jenny's school report "purposefully hurting themselves without wanting to die." This is from the state of Vermont's 2015 Youth Risk Behavior Survey data, a nationwide survey conducted every other year by the National Centers for Disease Control. In this same survey, more girls than the state average report prolonged feelings of sadness or hopelessness, and a higher than average percentage report having made suicide plans.[8]

In this same school, a girl named Karen once made a film about depression. It was her culminating product in a year-long, high school documentary film class, co-taught by a health teacher and an English teacher. The mission of the class was for students to identify a challenge facing teens in the community, to illuminate that challenge, and to document the resources in the community available to help young people persevere.

The teachers regularly brought guests into the class, experts discussing their work in the community and others sharing testimonials of hardship and overcoming. The English teacher, David, remembers the day when Karen, a hyper-guarded, quiet girl, told the class about where she cut her own body and how nobody knew except her parents.

"Actually," says David, "it was less the class that Karen told, though all of us were there." Rather, David explains, Karen was looking in the eyes of another young woman, a few years older than her, a guest who had come to the class that day with her therapist, a community-based mental health counselor. David and his colleague had invited this counselor to talk to the class about teen depression, a topic of interest to the students. Fortunately, the counselor had a client, several years out of high school by that time, who was willing to publicly talk about her journey.

Karen must have heard elements of her own journey reflected in the mirror of this other young woman's story, coaxing her own story to break through a silence. Karen's comfort in discussing her own struggles, and those endured by other young people she knew, only increased as the year went on. By the end of the year, Karen had made a documentary film about teenage depression:

There are the sounds of rain in the opening frames, then a title card, and then Karen's camera turns over the rail of a bridge. We see a waterfall, the crashing cold water below. Then Karen shows an ambulance, the image is filtered to black, white, and grays. Lights flashing, the ambulance is parked along the main street in town. She cuts away from the ambulance to a statistic about untreated depression being the leading cause of suicide, third leading cause of death among teenagers. Back to the ambulance, a car rolls slowly past. She has slowed the speed of the film to half. The lights flash slowly in black and white. Another statistic tells how few teenagers ever try to get help with their depression. Back to the silent ambulance, another car slowly drives by. Another statistic tells how depression is closely associated with antisocial and self-destructive behaviors, such as alcohol and drug abuse. She zooms in on the ambulance, closer, the lights slowly flashing in silence.

The first people to speak in Karen's film are experts from the local mental health center. Testimonials of youth come next. The first interviewee sits on her bed, facing a camera on a tripod. Her first words are "You're in this hole." It's Karen. The text across the screen identifies her, and under her name, "Filmmaker."

"You're in this hole, where you don't care about anything. You just feel sad all the time, and it's more of just . . . a sadness. And feeling that you just couldn't get out of it." A black kitten struts across the bed, small and goofy. Karen seems not to notice. Karen's eyes and face are open and bright, earnest and looking directly into the camera. There is no hair half-draped over her face as there is so often in school. There is no downward slouch. She is looking up and open; a filmmaker telling her story.

In addition to sharing her own story, Karen interviews several other girls, some anonymously, some with their voices or faces obscured—but each of them telling elements of their life story to the world. In the final minutes of the film, the girls and adults talk about what to do if one is experiencing depression. Karen's voice is the last voice: "Go to somebody that you trust, somebody who genuinely cares about what you feel. Go to them." She concludes her film by sharing a short list of hotline phone numbers for depression and suicide prevention. This information overlays pictures of the river again, not the crashing waters with which she'd opened, but a calm pool, farther downstream where someone is fishing in the quiet water.

"HE GRABBED HER LEFT FOREARM"

In the same school where David co-taught the documentary film class, he once had a student named Lori in English class. It was an October day devoted to writing first drafts of original stories when David looked up and didn't see Lori in the room. He asked a student, who said Lori had just stepped out into the hallway.

She was just outside the door, on her laptop, engrossed in her writing, head down, fingers clacking on the keyboard. David checked in, asked how the drafting was going, and reminded Lori to electronically share the document with him before the end of the day. A few hours later, a Google Doc appeared in David's inbox.

When David opened the document he saw, below the title of the story, a warning to the reader: "Caution: contains conversation about self-harm." Reading on, David discovered a story thematically entwined with the life Lori was living, and seeing lived, outside of school.

Lori's story is about a seventeen-year-old girl, Carly, and an eighteen-year-old boy, JJ, who is "walking the streets" in town, a week out of rehab after confronting his struggles with heroin:

> It's really hot sunny. JJ thought to himself, "I'm feeling pretty good since I went and got help." JJ accidentally bumped into an old friend, Carly Davis.
> Carly looked at JJ and said "JJ? That you?"
> JJ looked at her and said, "Carr! Omg! How are you?!" JJ told Carly how it was in rehab.
> "Wow. I can't believe it's been 11 months since you left! It seems like it's been forever," said Carly.

JJ's been gone for almost a year. Before he went to rehab, every time he saw Carly, he felt butterflies in his stomach. JJ really likes Carly, but he doesn't know how to tell her. JJ's had a crush on Carly since he was 15, and she was 14. They were both in 8th grade when they met. He thought she was just absolutely gorgeous. She has blue eyes, and really dark-brown hair. JJ, he has brown eyes, and dirty-blonde hair. JJ's now 18, and Carly's 17. Carly's had a crush on JJ as well, she just never could figure out how to tell him. She thought everything about JJ was perfect. From the way he laugh to the way he got into mischief.

Later in the story, the two friends are hanging out. Carly has graduated from high school, has a job, has an apartment, and pays the rent. She generously offers to take JJ shopping at Walmart to get some new clothes:

As they were walking, JJ noticed something on Carly's wrist . . . he was a little concerned. He thought to himself "I must be seeing things" but he took a second look and realized what he was seeing were what seemed to be cuts. He looked at Carly with a concerned facial expression and asked, "Carly . . . what's this?" and grabbed her left forearm.

Carly looked at the ground and pulled her arm back, "Nothing," she said.

He looked at her and knew she was scared of what he might say if she told him. JJ pulled up his sweatshirt sleeve revealing scars from his past.

This writing assignment was a very open-ended one. The content and themes were left to the students to decide. The teacher, David, created the conditions that helped Lori feel safe exploring the themes and content of her own life, even those themes she thought were raw enough to require a warning to her reader.

Lori's female character is, in part, a projection of whom Lori hopes to become, what she wants for herself now or in the future. Her character is a young woman able to support herself independently in the world, paying rent and holding down a job, and she meets someone with whom she can share the story of her struggles—and who will share his story with her.

Lori's story also reminds us that boys cut, too. In fact, in the same documentary film class where Karen made the film about teen depression, on the same day when she spoke about self-harm, a boy in the class also revealed how he sometimes engages in self-harm, except with fire: a lighter held under his forearm, or a candle.

Yet, while self-harm and suicide are themes in the lives and stories of boys—indeed, more boys and men kill themselves than do girls and women[9]—the themes of depression, self-harm, and suicide intertwine more often in the stories written by the girls in this school than in the boys' stories. It is harm to others—fighting—that is more often a theme in the stories written by boys. In the Youth Risk Behavior Survey, twice as many boys in the school report having been in a fight in the last twelve months.[10] This is not to say girls don't fight—and one might ask Lori about that.

The same year she was working on her story about heroin and cutting, Lori was punched in the face by another girl, Sonia, who'd walked into Lori's science class to confront her about lies she'd heard Lori was telling. When Lori stood up, Sonia hit her.

Until that day, adults in the school had heard Sonia posturing about hitting others, saying she wasn't afraid to fight. But until that day, she had never been in a physical confrontation in school. Sonia's counselor and the principal had talked to her about how to de-escalate tension, and told her she could—and should—come tell them if she ever felt on the verge of conflict. She got into the habit of coming to see her principal or counselor at lunch, sometimes just to say hello, sometimes with strong feelings she needed to express. If there was tension with a peer, they would discuss the possibility of mediation to ease the tension, but Sonia always vehemently refused the idea of talking face-to-face with those she had been insulted by or insulted. "They're not worth it," she would say. By which, perhaps, Sonia also meant, "I'm not worth it."

The school suspended Sonia for hitting Lori, and there followed several post-suspension restorative justice meetings. These meetings, to the adults' surprise, led Sonia to express interest in a mediation with Lori. The adults were proud of her for taking this step. It felt like progress. Then suddenly, the next week, Sonia stopped coming to school. She had attempted suicide and was hospitalized.

"I HAVE SO MUCH TO SAY"

Jenny, Karen, Lori, and Sonia are girls in rural, mostly white, small towns at a time when national data tells us that life expectancy for non-Hispanic whites is—like the title of Jenny's poetry Google Doc—going down. This decline in life expectancy is a result of suicide, alcoholism, and drug overdose.[11]

Economic factors exacerbate these trends, and these trends exacerbate the normal challenges of adolescence. It's hard to grow up when the adult world around you is crumbling down. And it's even harder when you feel you have to keep the pain bottled up inside, or when your only outlets are the risky online platforms of social media.

"Young Adults as Likely to Die from Suicide as from Traffic Accidents" was the title of a 2016 article in the *New York Times* that named social media as a major factor in the increasing suicides of kids in their early teens. At the same time that traffic-related fatalities were going down for this age group, young girls were taking their own lives at an increasing rate. The author notes, "The number is an extreme data point in an accumulating body of evidence that young adolescents are suffering from a range of health problems associated with the country's rapidly changing culture."[12]

Social media is a significant factor in the changing culture, with one factor being how easy it can be to make someone feel shame: "The pervasiveness of social networking means that entire schools can witness someone's shame." Amplifying feelings of shame can be deadly, and "social media tends to exacerbate the challenges and insecurities girls are already wrestling with at that age."[13]

In this light, it was a good thing that the girl with the pencil sharpener blades took her friend to the bathroom. Rather than simply posting her feelings, deeds, or intentions on social media, she shared with one friend, in person. There was no other audience that could, with a click, worsen the shame and pain. And these two girls were in a school, in the company of adults whom the friend knew would respond appropriately if they were informed.

In addition to helpful peers and adults who will react when they hear the stories, our young people need teachers and other adults who will *ask* for their stories, and model how to tell personal stories. This conveys to these youth that their words have worth, that what's inside matters, and that adults can help their stories be told.

In Jenny's poem, which opened this chapter, she is very eloquent—and yet she is still asking for help in telling her story: "I have so much to say, / But I can't seem to find the words." Better we help her find the words, and that they be spoken in safe and supportive spaces, with adults who care to listen. Better they be written in ink than in blood.

QUESTIONS FOR REFLECTION AND DISCUSSION

1. What are the youth who speak in this chapter telling us about why they harm their bodies?
2. In your own community, consider the ways that young people engage in harmful or unhealthy behaviors. If these behaviors are efforts to communicate something important, what are these behaviors asking or saying?
3. Does your community or school invite young people to express their thoughts and feelings, even when those thoughts and feelings are dark or difficult to hear? In what ways are your efforts in this area effective, or not?
4. What models do young people in your community have of people who are maturely and confidently reflecting on the struggles they have endured?

Chapter Two

SWAGGER

How can one dream of power . . . in any other terms than the symbols of power?

—James Baldwin, *The Fire Next Time* [1]

In times of normal adolescent identity uncertainty, many young men can find identity certainty in the modes and themes of the dominant culture, including masculine bravado, degradation of women, and violence.

Indeed, harming others and breaking things is one way that adolescents can impact the world and gain a sense of self and power. Violence is a way for adolescent aggression and rebellion to do its work. But there are better ways. Young people can also dismantle things with the power of their ideas, by wielding their ideals as tools to break things through meaningful critique and revolt. This requires confrontation with substantive adult perspectives in matters of moral and political significance.

Alas, the immaturity and nihilism of mainstream adult culture today make this hard. It's hard to be an adolescent when the dominant adult culture is itself so adolescent: aggressively self-centered, impulsive, and pleasure-seeking.

In one of the oldest of stories there is evil and upheaval in youth. The Old Testament tells of young Cain, who kills Abel. Then violence spreads across the land, and soon God brings the flood. When the waters recede, upon smelling the odor of Noah's sacrifices, the Lord says he "will never again curse the ground because of man" because, he says, "the imagination of man's heart is evil from his youth." [2]

Though we may not call it evil, the violent imaginations and deeds of youth are familiar to those who work with adolescents. These are age-old stories we see told every new day. Familiar, but still the violence can be unsettling.

Even mission-driven professionals who dedicate themselves to working with young people in times of trouble can find themselves needing distance from the volatility and aggression. "Kids these days," we may lament, and seek distance from their disruptions: their loud calls, the boys in the hall, their hard stares, the girls, their glares and nails, the scrawling on the chair, the dissonance and piercings, the tears and accusations, the closed door and open challenge, broken glass.

But though we may want or need distance, it is important that we return to listen, and listen closely.

In a school community much different from the one Jenny, Lori, and Karen attended, there once was a student named Jeremiah. He often wore red and he said very little else, as the red spoke his allegiances, flagging his affiliations in neighborhoods and streets divided. That he said little spoke to a need: a need for his teachers to reach out to him. And when they did, he had plenty else to say.

He came to school one day with a massive stack of paper, a collection of his own writings: poems, raps, letters, journal entries, and more. He was about fifteen years old, and there were about fifteen teachers at this small New York City public school for transfer students—young people who, for various reasons, were looking for another chance at graduation in a smaller, more communal and personalized setting.

During the few months he was in attendance, Jeremiah had begun to open up, in art class and in advisory especially. He'd begun to trust the adults, and due to circumstances in life outside school he was facing a court date, perhaps time in a residential or incarcerated school setting. But he didn't want to leave this school before sharing more of who he was. He brought the stack of papers to school, proud of all he'd written. One of the entries is titled "Phone Numbers 3:05 AM."

> Shorty let me get ya number I might call you
> Driving in my hummer
> Catch a date
> Put ya head down
> Get a taste
> Wat I got
> Is straight face to face
> Kill you
> Spray you with the 8
> Yea call me
> I got weight
> And I [got] weed
> Be on the tour bus
> Smoking trees

Just say please
Have my seed
(Chorus):
Shorty
Give me ya phone number
And I'll call
Just for date and we
Could ball
Damn dog
These ho's all over me
Roll up this Christmas tree
Smoke it don't loc it
I'll kill you
Right in public
Me and my nigga
Came ready to ride
And we ready to die
All [the] [damn] time
As we multiply
Dog we don't cry
Listen up

What do we hear in these lyrics, this story? Is it fact or fantasy? Remembrance or projection? Where does it come from? He drives a Hummer in this story, a symbol of war and wealth. He describes oral sex in the vehicle and rhymes on about killing her or someone, and guns, dope, and not crying. There's a fearlessness of dying, allusions to fame and immortality, and words like "dog" and "ho" and "kill" and "multiply." Whether it is real or imagined, it is harsh, and many adults may want to distance themselves from it. But we should listen.

Part of listening, of course, is at the level of first response, assessing whether there is immediate danger. Teachers who encounter visions of violence in the writing of students must inquire to ensure the child is not actually in danger or posing a danger to others. School counselors and social workers may need to be consulted; protocols for reporting and procedures for ensuring the safety of the child must be followed. But in addition to these basic measures, we must also listen to the stories of identity-striving that speak underneath—and wrestle with how they connect to the broader culture to which we all belong.

DROWNING IN ITSELF

There is an essay by Friedrich Nietzsche in which he writes of the destructive force of youth. He is writing to and about academia, to historians in particular, declaring the need for youthful energy to disrupt their ivory tower inertia and relativism. He is calling for the "rude willing and desiring" of youth,[3] the energy of young people who "are not yet old and wise enough to know their place," whose mission is to "shake" present-day concepts of health and education, who "generate ridicule and hatred," who offend with their indifference toward what is well known or established, "even toward much that is good."[4]

Jeremiah certainly seems indifferent toward goodness in his rhymes. In these next lyrics, he writes of killing a man and woman in their bed:

> Light up a blunt
> Shoot and run
> Not me
> I put a couple more
> Holes in him
> Make sure he dead
> Yea the job is done
> Call me OG
> Tell him
> Yea the job is done
> And that nigga had a son
> Lord you gotta forgive
> Me
> He [try] to kill me
> Fuck I shot him in the
> Head
> Baby moms too
> Both laid down in the bed
> Bleeding dead meat
> Off ya feet
> Put him down in the street

The protagonist in this short story is someone who refuses to back down, who chooses violence as his response, who kills his enemy and kills again, taking the life of an innocent, and along the way asks God for forgiveness. These violent visions—"bleeding dead meat"—may sound like indifference toward conventional morality, but in fact Jeremiah is speaking sentiments and signs that are not so different from those of his nation's dominant society. Jeremiah, like most children, is writing his identity with the words and images he has been given, the rude willing and desiring that is inherent in the broader cultural and political experience of our country. Jeremiah rhymes a rawer, but still true, rendering of certain mainstream American values.

Consider what gets valued in "Phone Numbers": a big car and material prowess, drugs or alcohol for pleasure and distraction, the sexual objectification of women and girls, male invulnerability and the gun, the public shaming and destruction of foes, the pursuit of fame and stardom. Jeremiah is simply revering what's revered. These are not fringe cultural trends or subcultural aspirations. These are the themes of television programs and advertisements on Sunday afternoons: the most popular, the best sellers, the chosen. Indeed, these are qualities that can get you elected president.

Various writers have compared the forty-fifth president to a teenager. Donald Trump's acute social status sensitivities, lack of historical sense, inflated self-importance, and impulsivity convey a developmental immaturity. During the presidential campaign, Mark Bowden, in *Vanity Fair*, shared impressions after spending a weekend with the future president: "Trump struck me as adolescent, hilariously ostentatious, arbitrary, unkind, profane, dishonest, loudly opinionated, and consistently wrong."[5]

Marwan Bishara, senior political analyst for *Al Jazeera*, wrote a piece during the first hundred days focused on "Trump's dangerous adolescence," observing a man "staying up late, watching videos" and sending tweets. Bishara asks, "Who but an adolescent snaps at trashy rumours and insinuations at 4 AM?" He notes how Trump seems to oscillate "like a pendulum between attention-seeking and utter insecurity; between 'me, me, me' and 'they all hate me.'" These are the symptoms, Bishara says, of "a troubled teenager: irritability, argumentativeness, defiance, and vindictiveness."[6]

Obviously, these are traits with which much of the U.S. electorate identifies, enough to see their values reflected in the man and to elect him to our highest office. What does this mean for our children? What does it mean for an actual adolescent, charting his or her path to maturity, when the president of the nation, and much of the country's adult culture, exhibit adolescent tendencies?

Jeremiah wasn't writing his rhymes of defiance, status-seeking, and explosiveness in the era of the Trump presidency, but he was living in a time when Trump's brand, books, and reality television shows were best sellers. Trump and Jeremiah are contemporaries, two New Yorkers striving for status within the same symbolic systems. In 2004, the same year Jeremiah shared his lyrics with his teachers, the fame-fetishizing *American Idol* topped the TV charts, and Donald Trump landed on those charts himself, launching the popular first season of *The Apprentice* to share his values and vision of leadership with the world.

The author and activist Naomi Klein has written about Trump's rise to power and "the stories and systems that ineluctably produced him." She reflects on popular culture and finds that, whether we like it or not, nearly all of us are swimming "in the cultural waters of reality TV and personal branding and nonstop attention-splintering messages—the same waters that produced Donald Trump."[7]

The adolescent adult culture is pervasive, and not new. The popular culture is rife with impulsive, youthful, unreflective action. Our nation's youth is thus drowning in itself—and this poses a developmental problem.

ADOLESCENT FORCE

To be young, self-centered, and without a sense of past—a personal, familial, communal, or societal past—is an unhealthy place to be. For without a communal past, without an inheritance of mature adult ideals to confront, with only the "me" and "here and now," the destructive force of youth has nothing substantive to dismantle—nothing, that is, but other people and themselves. Our society is not giving Jeremiah the right material on which to work his adolescent force. Instead of wielding the power of youthful idealism to attack injustices, such as the inequities that engender desperate struggles for resources in the streets where he roams, Jeremiah wields (or imagines wielding) a gun, his bullets tearing into human meat.

This is one of the dangers that comes with denying our young people a mature cultural inheritance transmitted by a mature adult culture. We are not channeling their youthful spirit in the direction of healthy rebellion or creative destruction. This is true of children no matter what community they live in, no matter what side of the tracks.

"OVERGROWN BOYS AND GIRLS"

The rich and poor of any society are cast in the same elemental metal, impressed on sister sides of the coins of a common realm. Jeremiah, though he is raised in a resource-poor urban environment, breathes the same pop cultural air found in most other American neighborhoods. A lack of historical sense and an immersion in present need and impulse satisfaction are essential components of this common culture. It is something that can make adults, in the eyes of youth, seem like "overgrown boys and girls," to borrow a phrase from Erik Erikson, a psychologist who wrote extensively about adolescent identity development. [8]

Working in the middle of the twentieth century, Erikson saw an adult culture still familiar to us today, one preoccupied with "a world of gadgetry and buying power," consumed with consumerism and distraction. [9] Erikson perceived an abdication of adult duty, an abdication of the "responsibility on the part of the older generation" to provide "those forceful ideals which must antecede identity formation in the next generation." And whether or not youth accept or reject those values is almost beside the point. The adult handing-down of forceful ideals is important—if "only so that youth can rebel against a well-defined set of older values." [10]

In other words, when an adolescent is born at the dawn of puberty, ready to begin testing the waters of adulthood, the adult world she or he encounters must contain certain mature statements of what is right and wrong, assertions of how things have been done and should be done. This can take many forms:

ritual, adage, myth, tradition, golden rules, commandments, laws. In schools, this can take the form of clearly articulated core values, and the exposure of young people to adults—including teachers—with strongly held beliefs that guide them in their life's path. Young people need to hear adult expressions of tradition and conviction in order to know where they have come from, to get their bearings on where they might go, and in order to question, rebel against, or reject that which is no longer right or suited to the present world.

NIHILISM OF A NATIVE SON

Immaturity is just one word to describe the problematic state of our broader adult culture. Nihilism is another. Cornel West uses the term to encapsulate an absence of love, hope, and meaning. Poet philosophers like Cornel West—and James Baldwin and others—are particularly important to consider in contemplating Jeremiah's writing because they speak specifically to America's adolescent proclivities and the struggle, especially of mainstream white America, to maturely acknowledge the past. You can hear it in Jeremiah's poems—the nihilist voice of an American native son. You can hear it in this poem, titled "That's How I Grew Up":

I stay fresh to death
New airmax
Just like climax
I grew up in the hood
Yea I was adopted
3 weeks old
Never seen a part of my family
When I tried everthing
Got shady
Blinded my eyes
Sometimes I cryed
Wondering why
It had to be like this
Why couldn't I just sip some
Chris
And chill all day
My moms don't even look
Like me
Christmas came around
I still put up the tree
Nothing under there for me
I was to bad
Stayed home and felt sad
(Chorus 3x):
I aint chose this life
This life chose me

Damn why can't I just be me
Indeed I had a seed
Now I got a little baby boy
Messed up like a toy

The nihilism is palpable in Jeremiah's lyrics. His family is eroded and he has no sense of familial inheritance. Alcohol and Cristal enable forgetting. He feels personally unworthy, undeserving of gifts. Rituals and religious holidays are empty of love and meaning. He is helpless and choiceless before circumstance and fate. He sees his progeny as a "messed up" replication of himself, worthless, not human, like a toy.

Cornel West believes that nihilism like this is a contemporary problem in black communities. The genius, West would say, of black generations that came before Jeremiah and his parents, was a capacity to build barriers against this sense of worthlessness and meaninglessness. The communities had the ability to protect their children, like Jeremiah, from spiritual emptiness, even in conditions of material deprivation and oppression.

But that "cultural armor," West writes, has lost or is losing its protective power: "We have created rootless, dangling people with little link to the supportive networks—family, friends, school—that sustain some sense of purpose in life."[11] He wonders what has changed.

West sees two significant factors in what has gone wrong for black communities in the later twentieth century: a "crisis in black leadership" and "the saturation of market forces and market moralities in black life."[12] And perhaps these two crises are linked: leaders of all types and of every racial identity—whether parents, pastors, politicians, or CEOs—can find themselves putting profits before people. It's an insidious, Faustian desegregation that seems to happen so inexorably over time in America: the integration of a people into the majority "market morality." As West remarks, this nihilism "is not confined to black America":

> Psychic depression, personal worthlessness, and social despair are widespread in America as a whole. The vast majority of citizens—struggling to preserve a livelihood, raise children, and live decent lives—are disillusioned with social forces that seem beyond their control. Just as in the black community, the saturation of market forces in American life generates a market morality that undermines a sense of meaning and larger purpose.[13]

HEDONISTIC PRESENT

One reason that American youth—but indeed people of any age group—are vulnerable to nihilism is because we increasingly live our individual stories and strive for meaning outside a generational narrative. Our identity journeys are individual treks rather than communal endeavors. Intergenerational communities are being dismantled. Our grandparents are increasingly grouped into homogenous homes of the aged, in the care of strangers; grandchildren are collected during the day in nurseries, also in the care of near-strangers; cousins, aunts, and uncles often live in separate regions, isolated nuclear families apart, pursuing down highways and cul-de-sacs the American dream of the fenced-in yard.

Plucked from the cycles and stories of generational unfolding, we are left alone, or in a family alone. We are left alone and come to believe that to get what I want—and to get it right now—is what life is all about. "The result," writes West, "is lives of what we might call 'random nows,' of fortuitous and fleeting moments preoccupied with 'getting over'—with acquiring pleasure, property, and power by any means necessary."[14] It can be heard in Jeremiah's poems, like these untitled poems:

> Yeah I leave you twitching
> Come on dog I'm listening
> All day just pissing
> And dipping
> With the dipset
> Ya heard
> Fly to they sky like a bird
> Yea that Jey coming thru
> Come back and blew
> Yea dog its true
> Sit down look at the diamond
> So icy
> So shiny
> Shiny shiny
> Icy icy
> Like papi fight me

> Let me in I got haze
> Happy days
> Go ahead dog
> I got shiny rings
> Glimmering things
> Get blang
> Get bang. . .
> I be with the Dipset
> Getting real checks
> Drag u down the steps
> Have fun with
> Then get
> Get this cash
> Get that quick cash
> Quick fast
> Jey is a rich ass nigga

Rymeing with gigga
(Chorus 3x):
Get that gat
Flip it back
Then get my crack
Heart attack
Heart attack

Gat is a gun. Shiny, shiny is the diamond. Crack is a drug, and selling it will make money with which to buy glimmering things. "Gigga" may be a reference to Jigga, the rap artist, Jay-Z. In the online "Urban Dictionary," "Dipset" is noted to have been the name of a rap group in Harlem at the time Jeremiah was writing these rhymes, and that to dip or dipset also refers to leaving a place. Indeed, we can hear fight or flight in these poems.

And we can hear a market morality's reverence for luxurious things. Flee your fear, leave the past, live for the now and the shiny, shiny. "In the American way of life pleasure involves comfort, convenience, and sexual stimulation," writes West. "Pleasure, so defined, has little to do with the past and views the future as no more than a repetition of a hedonistically driven present."[15] And with this we come to our nation's lack of historical sense, at the heart of which, in the dominant American narrative, is denial:

> The American democratic experiment is unique in human history not because we are God's chosen people to lead the world but because of our refusal to acknowledge the deeply racist and imperial roots of our democratic project. We are exceptional because of our denial of the antidemocratic foundation stones of American democracy. No other democratic nation revels so blatantly in such self-deceptive innocence, such self-paralyzing reluctance to confront the nightside of its own history.[16]

West puts it in developmental terms:

> This sentimental flight from history—or adolescent escape from painful truths about ourselves—means that even as we grow old, grow big, grow powerful, we have yet to grow up. To confront the role of race and empire is to grapple with what we would like to avoid.[17]

QUEST FOR DIGNITY AND LOVE

Jeremiah at fifteen is just a year older than James Baldwin's nephew when Baldwin wrote the boy a letter on the occasion of the nation's "one hundredth anniversary of the emancipation." The letter is the first essay in a book that troubled and inspired the nation, *The Fire Next Time*. It is 1963, and Baldwin writes to his nephew in an effort to offer some of that protection Cornel West saw in earlier African American generations: cultural continuity, and the creation and preservation of hope through love.

In his letter, Baldwin writes of the boy's father, mentions his father's father's journey, and concludes with an assertion of the boy's ancestral belonging to a long line of great poets, quoting him a verse: "The very time I thought I was lost, My dungeon shook and my chains fell off."[18] It was an effort to protect and empower the boy, to fortify him with love and with the wisdom of elders, what they have learned about what it takes to live in this country as a black person among whites. He names white America's innocence, which is a mixture of denial and fear: denial of history and fear of losing an identity based on a myth of white superiority, white supremacy.

Moreover, as Baldwin writes in another essay, white American identity is not only grounded in the obvious and essential denial of the oppression of peoples upon which the United States was founded and grew. This white American identity also thrives on a denial of the real reasons Europeans came here in the first place. White Americans, Baldwin suggests, deny the past not only because of shame for sins committed—slavery, genocide—but because whites are also ashamed of what most whites *were* upon arrival to America: poor, oppressed, and rather wretched:

> the white American has never accepted the real reasons for his journey. I know very well that my ancestors had no desire to come to this place: but neither did the ancestors of the people who became white and who require of my captivity a song. They require of me a song less to celebrate my captivity than to justify their own.[19]

The history of our country shows that the European of many a color and hue became, in America, white—in order to become, at least, better than *some*body. This is the "price the white American paid for his ticket," a price many found worth paying: all the suffering is worth it if you can claim you're better than the black.[20] Baldwin asserts a desperate unwillingness in white America to go back and re-examine its past:

> To do your first works over means to reexamine everything. Go back to where you started, or as far back as you can, examine all of it, travel your road again and tell the truth about it. Sing or shout or testify or keep it to yourself: but *know from whence you came.* . . . This is precisely what the generality of white Americans cannot afford to do.[21]

Well, actually, much of white America can afford it, materially speaking. White America has command of extraordinary material resources, and deploys that material wealth and cultural capital every day to build buffers against the truth about the past. As long as the emotional and material levees that repress the flood tides of history still hold strong in white America, then, in the short term, white Americans can pretend they can afford it, spending great sums to keep the self innocent and keep history quiet. And even those who are not white can join in and sing the chorus of Jeremiah's song: shiny, shiny, fight me, fight me. Anytime shopping, perpetual war, perpetual now. West reminds us that "this culture engulfs all of us—yet its impact on the disadvantaged is devastating, resulting in extreme violence in everyday life," with the "most obvious signs" of an "empty quest for pleasure, property and power" embodied in "sexual violence against women and homicidal assaults by young black men on one another."[22]

This is the world in Jeremiah's rhymes, a world difficult to acknowledge and often hard to hear. The pain beneath the violence is especially hard to hear. It is hard to listen to pain when it speaks from behind masks of menace and bravado.

But if adults who maintain the distance can somehow better listen, we will hear that beneath the violence and quest for pleasure, there's really pain and a quest for dignity and love. Jeremiah is only fifteen—fifteen years old, this boy who writes of killing and conquest. And in the handwritten copy he shared of his poems and raps, one can see the print of a younger schoolboy. He dots his i's with circles and sometimes stars. He writes about his mother ("To My Momma"):

> She brong me up
> Bently big body truck
> My momma gave me everything
> It so good
> I thought it was dream
> Just like in the hood
> My momma cook for me
> Set up the Christmas tree
> When I dip and dive
> Thru the hood
> Its mine
> All day yea stay with the nine
> My moms told me no
> Pops said soo so
> He used to beat me
> Come back maybe see me
> (Chorus 2x):
> I love u momma
> Love u dear sweet momma
> Just sit back
> While I love you momma
> Even though my momma
> Want me locked up

Jeremiah brought the pages to school in a folder; some were stapled together into separate booklets. There were about a hundred pages in all, written in pen and pencil on wide-ruled school paper. He wanted to share it because the adults were starting to listen—and also, he liked to perform. But sharing his work wasn't performance this time. He was carrying a year or two of his life's work into the school office, making an offering of voice to people who would listen—on the eve of a court date and likely remand to a juvenile detention setting.

Jeremiah was proud of the quality and the content: the number of pages, and what he thought were very good rhymes. Other kids thought so too, apparently. Students in the school affirmed his skills as a rapper. And there was a letter in the stack from his girlfriend, which he also pointed out to his teachers, proud of her pride in him.

Jeremiah invited his teachers to read it all. His English teacher told him that if he wished, he could make a photocopy on the school copier, since this was his original and only draft. The teacher did it for him and gave his original back. He was soon removed from his home, and the school. The following poem is titled "Life in Jail":

> Yo this how they do it in jail
> Take a can full of beans
> Smash it up like a fean
> Then throw it [in] a sack
> Bang u with it
> Shit felt like a rock
> Cause when I was locked up
> Sitting in my cell
> All day
> The cops ringing the bell
> Lunch time
> Somebody getting sliced
> Bloody ass face
> Spray you with some mace
> (Chorus 3x):
> Locked up locked up
> Behind the bars
> Damn no more cars
> Locked up locked up
> When I got locked
> Niggas put blood on my paper
> Big ass red marker
> That shit will shape ya
> So they put [me] in crip city just like bigg[ie]
> Only one homie with me
> True story

What of all that he writes is fantasy, and what is true story? His teachers didn't know him well enough to say. But these were the stories he gave them to read. This is the story his country gave him. And these many pages of his, excerpted here, include raps, some with titles and some without; prose text without headings; lists of items in clothing lines he might sponsor; lists of songs on various albums in a series. In addition to dotting each "i" with a circle, any "c" has a line down through it, like a cent-coin sign. Sometimes an "s" reads like a dollar sign. His spelling has largely been left as written.

The last excerpt from Jeremiah's compilation shared here is the letter he included from his girlfriend, Nicole. The tenderness in her voice contrasts with the violence of his lyrics:

> Dear: Jeremiah a.k.a. my husband
> Baby, why are you so insecure? You know I'm not gonna cheat on you whether you're in jail or not. Nobody can ever treat me better than you. So *don't worry.* I love you and only you. But you're not going to jail anyway, so stop worrying yourself. And seriously, I'm going to stop fighting and arguing with people because I don't want you to start arguing and fighting too.
>
> I really want to get you out of New York. I want you to see and experience new things. But please baby, just be patient. You know I'm gonna take care of you. I hope you're record label goes through. But I know it's gonna go through. I'm really proud of you. You really are starting to change. I hate the fact that I don't live across the street from you anymore.

Like Jeremiah's rhymes, these words were handwritten in a young person's script on wide-ruled school composition paper. One can't understand all of the references and intimacies she shares, but the force of her caring is clear. She recalls visiting him once in the hospital and worries about losing him: "You can rap, you can draw, you learn very quickly. Baby, you are truly one-in-a-million. You are too smart to let all of that go to waste." She recalls a dangerous time around Christmas:

> I still can't believe you got shot at on Christmas Eve. That day after we all opened our Christmas gifts, and everyone went to sleep. And I was laying on your chest, I started crying. Just thinking about you not hear really made me brake down. I'm getting sad just thinking about it. Nobody will ever love you the way I love you. You're my everything.

She shares other reflections: on fidelity, love, and the dangers they face and must surmount. At the end of her letter she describes sitting next to a young child as she writes, envisioning her future with Jeremiah:

> Right now, Daniel is staring at me while I'm writing. Looking at him always makes me think about the children we'll have one day. But when we both are working and stuff because I don't want us to struggle anymore. Baby please just understand that.
>
> It seems like yesterday when you were trying to get with me. Now we're in love planning our future. Well, I think I wrote enough. I love you Jeremiah.

"I love you, Jeremiah." That's the heart of it. This young woman is trying—as was James Baldwin with his letter—to love the boy, to protect him, to give him hope. She's trying to imagine for him a future that isn't death too soon, that is relationship to another, that is family, good work, calm, and trust.

In his songs Jeremiah prophesies jail or death and, sadly, he's just seeing the writing on the wall, playing the odds. Nicole is writing against the odds, writing with the best memory and nostalgia and kindness that she can call forth—to write him, and her, something else.

Love. West would say it is the answer: "Nihilism is not overcome by arguments or analyses; it is tamed by love and care."[23] Baldwin says it also. He wrote this to his nephew, and to Jeremiah:

> Well, you were born, here you came, something like fifteen years ago . . . here you were: to be loved. To be loved, baby, hard, at once, and forever, to strengthen you against the loveless world. Remember that: I know how black it looks today, for you. It looked bad that day, too, yes, we were trembling. We have not stopped trembling yet, but if we had not loved each other none of us would have survived. And now you must survive because we love you, and for the sake of your children and your children's children.[24]

Love. Any other response seems inadequate. What else can be said other than *love him*? If we take Jeremiah at his word—true story or fantasy is of no matter, for it is real because it is valued—then what he needs is love—from others, for others, and for himself. He was adopted, has no sense of familial past, has a mother in whom he cannot see himself—who wants him to go to jail—and a father he remembers for his violence. Jeremiah believes he is too bad to deserve presents at Christmas. He has a gun, a fist, a knife, scars, and wounds and the will to inflict the same. He's got blood of women and men on his hands, jail in his past and future, slurs and degradation ever on the tip of his tongue. He is claiming and speaking that glorified American insatiable thirst for anonymous sex, violence, money, cars, speed, drugs, and fame: your name in shiny shiny gold upon the tower.

But really what Jeremiah wants is respect, and dignity, and some honor. And really, also, he wants to be forgiven. And he wants to have a business. And he's only fifteen. And he wants to have his pain and loss acknowledged. Rather, he *needs* to have his pain and loss acknowledged.

His girlfriend, in her letter, is trying to offer him the kind of love that Jeremiah also needs the adults of his world to provide. She talks of listening to him: staying up late and just talking. She asks him to control his destructive impulses. She envisions a future for him. She reminds him of the past. This is the work that the adults in his world must do, and schools can play a part. Alas, Jey was only in the small community-minded school a short while. His teachers were only able to do the first thing, and only briefly: to briefly be with him and listen.

QUESTIONS FOR REFLECTION AND DISCUSSION

1. What do Jeremiah's lyrics make you think or feel? What do you think Jeremiah is communicating with these rhymes?
2. How do the youth you know communicate or act in ways that contrast with notions of propriety and ethical behavior? How does your school or wider community respond to youth who act in such ways?
3. Do you agree that mainstream adult culture in the United States has adolescent or immature traits? Why or why not?
4. Do the observations of Cornel West and James Baldwin shared in this chapter align or diverge with how you understand our country? What does or doesn't resonate with you?

Chapter Three

STUMBLE

I thought [that] putting the bullet on the bible
would purify the dreams and grudge.

—Roberto, "Hollow Point"

Adolescents growing up in a time of tumult and uncertainty can find certainty in concrete acts of violence toward self or others. But physical harm to self and others isn't a path chosen by most. There are other paths. Unfortunately, the identity narratives we offer our young people are often too numerous, open-ended, and confusing. The path toward identity coherence becomes cluttered, interrupted, broken. Youth will stumble along instead of stride strong. This is yet another challenge faced by young people growing up in a world of globalized media, constant interruptions, and innumerable cultural intersections. Too much meaning can sometimes be as great a challenge as not enough.

"That shit will shape ya," Jeremiah rhymes—and he's not talking about school. In another verse he reminds, "I aint chose this life / This life chose me." He's right, of course. Many circumstances coalesce in the world to choose a child's path well before that child is even born. And then life chooses the child, the child is born, and then a lot happens from year one to five that shapes that child before he or she even gets to kindergarten.

Yet, even after all that happens, the years that follow school are an important part of any individual's journey. If Jeremiah had found his way to a good school for more than a few months, his rhymes could have been made to resonate within walls of reflection—within the confines of community—rather than the concrete confines of incarceration.

In the right school setting, for a long enough amount of time, Jeremiah's past could be acknowledged and valued, and he would come to understand, through his studies, the broader and deeper past that has shaped him. He would study historical forces and facts. He would come to understand that the trouble around him is not his fault and that he can help fix it. He would find his place in a community where his words hurt if they are insulting, where he is reprimanded and allowed to earn forgiveness. He would encounter values that cohere with the core human values that shape his own buried sense of guilt and worth.

In other words, Jeremiah would begin to have a better sense that there is something eternal and good, that it has to do with trust and love more than it has to do with fame and shiny things—and he would start to see that he's a part of it. Schools can make a difference in the life of a child, even someone in their mid- to late teens.

Nevertheless, educators and all citizens must search for earlier interventions and broader economic and political solutions: mothers and fathers of every social stratum deserve living-wage work, secure housing, and health care—before the child's birth and into the elementary years. And we must help communities maintain meaningful intergenerational public spaces and institutions—religious and secular—to support the family and the child's early development.

And our schools must be extensions of these spaces. They are out there. In such schools we can find essential ingredients of sound adolescent identity development, elements of that cultural armor that Cornell West sees rusting and failing. Such schools offer youth community, continuity, and the opportunity to channel their pain, aggression, and questions in ways that foster healthy personal and social change, not self-destruction.

ONE TO HOLD A DOOR OPEN

At a small New York City public school, similar to the one Jeremiah attended, was a teenage boy, Roberto. He had transferred from a Catholic high school in the middle of his high school years. The principal, Mr. Harrison, would get to know him well.

At first, their conversations had nothing to do with distress or discipline. Roberto might stop by Mr. Harrison's office during lunch to offer a cordial greeting. He was a young man with an almost gentlemanly way, with goodwill and gentility. He was one to hold a door open.

Mr. Harrison's first impression was of a sixteen-year-old boy burdened and blessed with sincerity and naiveté. Socially, at lunch and in the hallways, he seemed to hover like a butterfly, but clumsy sometimes. Not a social butterfly—rather like a hummingbird, hovering and then darting in, maybe bumping with his shoulders. He had broad shoulders. He had kind intentions but was unsure of his role and place, ever ready with a faux pas, maybe stepping on your sneaker.

Along with peer relationships, Roberto struggled with norms of student-teacher interactions. Roberto once visited Mr. Harrison during lunchtime. At one point they were discussing a *Calvin and Hobbes* book Roberto had taken out of his bag and put on the table—those cartoons of a brazen little boy and his play tiger friend. Mr. Harrison told him he had always liked the cartoons, especially the ones about sledding and snowballs. Roberto handed his principal the book and said it was his to keep. It was a nice gesture, but atypical behavior. Roberto smiled tentatively and insisted his principal keep the book as a gift.

Roberto's smiles were usually tentative, a lovely smile beneath round cheeks, nose, and glasses. He would smile and then he would turn his face and eyes away, not entirely at ease in a direct gaze. He wore a lot of khaki, earth colors of muted tones. Roberto was a sheltered boy who therefore needed sheltering more, needed some protecting and guiding—so that something didn't go wrong as he moved awkwardly but softly through a sometimes brutal city and the often brutal time called adolescence.

A MACHO DECREE

Roberto was in Tina's advisory group with about thirteen other students for whom Tina, a young math teacher, served as first resource for academic and personal guidance. In the middle of Roberto's first year at the school, Tina came into Mr. Harrison's office with Roberto at lunchtime.

Roberto sat at the table with ice on a swollen lip, blood on the paper towel covering the ice pack. He'd been punched in the face outside the deli where students go for sandwiches at lunch. The boy who had hit him no longer attended the school, but had been a student for some time. He was among the most disenfranchised, a young man poorly served by past schools and by a neglectful society. His name was Floyd, and words were like enemies. He didn't like them. Spoken to, he would go silent quickly, clenching fists if frustrated, or silently searching for a word of reply.

Floyd had built relationships with a few teachers. He wanted to do well, to graduate. But he was in his late teens, and school had become too corrosive to Floyd's sense of self-worth. More and more of the words and skills he was supposed to possess, he didn't. Fourteen-year-olds were surpassing him. The supports the school could offer him—and his mother—were not enough at his age. At a meeting Mr. Harrison once had with his mother and sister, they confessed their fear of Floyd's bouts of anger. They worried for their safety. There seemed to be none of what a family would need to cope, such as church community, extended family, or the resources to send him elsewhere for help or care. There was a small, caring school, yes, but it was a long subway ride away, and he was disengaging. Soon after that school meeting with his mom, Floyd stopped attending school and then dropped out, at nineteen, with the credits of a ninth grader. By the time Roberto was enrolled, Floyd was still coming by the school—but only to see his girlfriend, Suzie.

Suzie and Roberto were in the same advisory group and saw each other every day. They got along, but Roberto didn't always know how to negotiate friendship at the appropriate distance. He would comment on things that a casual friend normally wouldn't, like her hair, her clothes, or where she shopped, recalling small details he might have overheard.

Suzie told Floyd that Roberto was "like, stalking me or something." He wasn't—but maybe he did have a crush. Or maybe he just thought she was a friend. Anyway, one day Suzie's boyfriend, Floyd, made a simple macho decree: Roberto must talk no more to Suzie.

Perhaps Roberto knew but didn't care, or forgot, or couldn't really believe Floyd was serious, but when Roberto saw Suzie and Floyd coming out of the deli at lunch, he said something to Suzie about her selection of Doritos. It was a simple remark about the type of chip she'd chosen, something like, "So you like Cool Ranch?"

Silently Floyd turned to him, no outward indication of his patience cracked, and asked, "Did you say something to my girl?" Roberto gave a sincere reply, without challenge or defense, "Yeah, I was asking about her chips." With this confirmed and without words, a stone-faced Floyd crushed Roberto's lips into his teeth.

BEWILDERED BY VIOLENCE

Floyd's face would change very little when he moved from ease to anger, a barely perceptible clouding of the brow. So on that white, sunlit October day, Roberto had no idea what was coming. Floyd's shoulders were narrower than Roberto's, and he stood a full foot shorter, but Roberto had no idea, no defensive stance, and, being no fighter, he was knocked down to the sidewalk. Then he got up, came inside, muddled and hurt, and told Tina.

He told Mr. Harrison, in the hours that followed, that he didn't want revenge. He didn't want to fight Floyd. This was one of the first things the principal tried to discover in a time of fresh conflict: how quickly was it going to get bigger? Would there be another, worse fight after school? What challenges and amplifications of challenges had been cast? What friends or family would get involved?

If Mr. Harrison had thought there was danger of escalation and actual violence in the school or streets, he would have immediately reached out to families and friends to express that the school had an expectation of nonviolence. There were families and students who would push back against the notion that school business extended to the streets and after-school hours, but the assertion at this small personalized school was that the "nexus" of the school included sites off school grounds if student interactions there were going to impact school life.

If there was concern over violence, Mr. Harrison would also alert police officers and school safety personnel whom he trusted, and ask them to deploy carefully at dismissal to help ensure safe passage from school to subway train and bus stop. Faculty would also step up to be a presence in the halls and outside, perhaps to walk with students to the train, or some might find reasons to keep a student after school to avoid the most crowded hours and most conflict-prone corners. If there was talk of payback, Mr. Harrison might also head to the subway or street corners, a presence himself that could help remind students of the school's expectations.

But Roberto seemed uninterested in payback. He seemed mystified. He said he didn't understand why it had happened. He described the incident in detail, haltingly, slowly, his lip puffed and cut. Mr. Harrison listened. Tina had already taken Roberto upstairs to the health clinic, and apparently his teeth were fine and there was no need to go to the hospital.

Imagine a big little boy (like Calvin from Calvin and Hobbes) unable to take his play tiger around with him anymore; who is sixteen and doesn't fit in, who is precocious enough only to be maladroit; who wants to have friends, a girlfriend, and wants things to be easy and peaceful and nice; a boy who used to wear a uniform and sit in rows, who comes to a new school and has no compass to help him navigate. Unable to read most signs, yet in this school he generally finds tolerance and acceptance, and does fine in his classes.

There are plenty of other social misfits at this transfer school, most of whom find each other—and even those who don't are given empathy and space, like Roberto. He now sat before Mr. Harrison and Tina bewildered by the violence just visited upon him by a wordless, expressionless force. Roberto looked at the blood on the paper towel when he pulled it from his lip, as if in wonder. He wasn't crying.

Where would he go with his feelings, and what were they? The scripts of group battle and stories of turf and color were foreign to him, so he wasn't calling for revenge or texting allies in his neighborhood to come down to meet the challenge. No, he came right inside and told a teacher, as a child might after being pushed by the bully at the swing at recess—or simply because he had no one else to tell. Tina, sitting there with him, had tearful eyes.

Mr. Harrison and Tina, with help from Celeste, a social worker who collaborated closely with the school, were able to resolve the conflict, outwardly. Suzie was willing to meet and mediate things with Roberto. She had been annoyed by him, but she also felt some shame at how brutally her boyfriend had behaved. And brutality like that is usually a problem for the girlfriend too—so there was likely some concern for herself as well. She didn't want to talk about it much, but she was able to restore things with Roberto, and the advisory group, enough to revive normalcy. In fact, aided by the social worker who'd worked with both boys, Roberto and Floyd met for a mediation too.

Floyd gave assurances that nothing else would happen. He admitted an unchecked angry impulse. Roberto's lip healed. At that point, Mr. Harrison wasn't worried about escalation. Floyd wasn't around that much, and Mr. Harrison trusted Floyd's assurances and how he too wished it hadn't happened. For Roberto, however, the story wasn't finished.

A BULLET

In the weeks following the incident with Floyd, Celeste had several meetings with Roberto, a continuation of consultations they'd begun earlier in the year. She didn't tell Mr. Harrison about what exactly they were discussing, but she did say there were great dramas playing out inside him. "A lot going on in there," she said. She was listening closely and carefully to his memories, reflections, and imagination. If she thought there was danger, she would tell Mr. Harrison, but for the moment she was just monitoring closely.

Winter recess came and went. In February, Celeste had to make a trip back to her childhood home in North Africa, to a small village where her father had died and where elaborate traditions of burial and passing required her presence. So Celeste wasn't around when Roberto gave his advisor, Tina, a bullet and told her, "I don't need this anymore." He refused to tell her anything else.

Tina didn't know what to do with it. She brought it to Mr. Harrison after school. That evening, Mr. Harrison called Roberto's mother. She was aware of the bullet. It had been given to Roberto by his sister's boyfriend, a cadet in the Police Academy. They discussed whether Roberto had access to a gun to shoot the bullet. She said no. She didn't understand why Roberto had brought it to school, but she thought it was a good idea to talk to him about it. She would talk to him too. With Celeste away, Mr. Harrison told Roberto's mom that he would meet with Roberto himself first thing the next day.

The next morning, when Roberto arrived, Mr. Harrison went to get Tina. The goal of the conversation was to better understand why he had brought the bullet to school, and why he had given it to Tina. Roberto talked about the bullet's hollow point, and why police officers had them, and how his sister's fiancé had given it to him. When Mr. Harrison asked directly why

Roberto had given it to Tina, he seemed unsure of what to say. In the silence that followed, Tina became visibly overwhelmed, tears in her eyes. At which point, Roberto, as if comforting a younger sister, put his hand on her shoulder and said, "It's OK. It's going to be OK." She took a breath and politely told him that he didn't need to tell her that.

"WRITE AT LEAST ONE PAGE"

Tina had to teach class, so she soon left the meeting. Mr. Harrison directed the conversation back to the bullet, and what meaning Roberto saw in it. Roberto wouldn't say much. He seemed surprised and betrayed by Tina's surrender of the object to the school administration.

Holding the bullet in his hand, Mr. Harrison told him, "This small object means nothing—and at the same time, Roberto, this bullet means a lot. It is harmless, in itself. Look at it, a little metal thing, small as the tip of my pinkie finger."

Roberto was looking at the object. Mr. Harrison asked him if he had a gun that could shoot it. He said no. He recounted again how his sister's boyfriend had given it to him.

Mr. Harrison told Roberto the importance of not bringing to school anything that could be a potentially dangerous object. Roberto agreed. Mr. Harrison asked directly about any plans to hurt himself or others. Roberto said no, and seemed to want to say little else. Mr. Harrison knew that Roberto had not fully explained what was going on inside, and with Celeste away he felt it was his role to find out more. He said Roberto would be allowed to go to class, but that it was important for Roberto to be willing to explore further and discuss what this object meant to him. He said that since Celeste was not present this week, Roberto would communicate with him instead. Roberto understood, but he registered some reluctance to discuss anything, now or later, with Celeste. He said she was getting too personal. Mr. Harrison noted that it was part of her job as a social worker to ask some personal questions.

Mr. Harrison gave Roberto an assignment: to write at least one page about what the object meant to him and why he gave it to Tina, due the next morning. Roberto agreed to do it. Mr. Harrison was curious to see what he would say, and decided to determine the next steps accordingly.

MEANING IN HOLLOW POINTS

Mr. Harrison could see three potential narratives sunk into Roberto's shiny little metal object: one wishing harm to other students, another about harming himself, and a third one somehow involving Tina. Roberto had told her he "didn't need it anymore." If indeed this was true, what had been the arrested intentions? Mr. Harrison felt he needed especially to know why Roberto had brought the bullet to school and given it to Tina. Perhaps what was today a bullet would tomorrow be a flower, some other symbol inappropriately applied, or perhaps a physical transgression. In the unsure self of this young man, had Tina assumed some exaggerated importance in his quest for self-definition?

The next morning Roberto turned in his writing assignment:

Hollow Point by Roberto F.
November, a few days before Thanksgiving.
It was a calm night, breeze felt good breathing on one's face. I was just getting home from a driving class. Tell you one thing, a five hour class listening about road hazards can really drain a person. Anyway it's a calm night and as I'm getting home, I see my friend walking toward me. It was Carla, a very nice friend of mine, she could be a bit of a cousin time to time. We came across each other a lot, but it was mostly during the daytime when the sun is still rising.

"Oh my God, I'm so glad to see you," I said.

"I'm coming back from work, anyway dude I'm so glad to see you!"

It was strange to hear those words from her. She sounded like I have been gone for thirty years. "What do you mean you are glad to see me? We saw each other yesterday morning," I said.

"Well, if you wanna know dude. I had a dream where you got shot. You died a painful death."

"Oh, that is pretty . . . messed up." Words failed to come to my head.

"It was so sad to see you in so much pain." She looked at me with a worried look. An expression that can stir someone in the inside.

"Well, usually when someone dreams about somebody else, it is because they came in contact with them." Thought that might calm her spirits.

"Oh, thank God. I was really worried."

"Hey, who can blame you."

After that conversation I got home. The thing that sparked me the most was that I had a dream too. Except I was being chainsawed to death. Knowing the feeling of a chainsaw going into your stomach, really can send chills down your spine. Then when you think it was just a dream, someone tells you that in their dream, I got killed. An hour later passes, the whole family is home including my sister's boyfriend. He was wearing a NYPD cap and under his shirt you can see the outline of the bulletproof vest.

"Hey dude what's good?"

"Hey Roberto. Nothing much really, just in training."

"Oh cool, man it is so cool you are going to be a cop."

"Yeah it's freakin awesome." He reached into his pocket and pulled out something. "Here I got you something."

I reached over and I was shocked to see what he gave me.

"It's a bullet," he said in a calm voice.

"Um yeah. I can see that."

"It's a police issued, nine millimeter hollow point bullet."[1]

"Yeah I've heard of this, but why use a hollow point instead of a regular bullet?"[2]

"Regular bullets would go through a target and cause minimum damage, which means less stopping power, while hollow points cause more tissue damage but will not go through a target."

The bullet felt a bit heavy in the palm of my hand. It was also smooth and shiny. It looked like it was fresh out of the box. The top of the bullet was hollowed out. It wasn't like a regular bullet at all.

It bothered me that a friend of mine had a dream of me dying, then I had a dream I was chainsawed. To death. Then after that my sister's boyfriend hands me over a bullet. It was cool looking at the bullet though. Still two dreams about death and then you get a bullet made the dreams look like conspiracy theories.

Mr. Harrison felt lucky that Roberto had been so forthcoming, that he'd taken to storytelling in response to the prompt. He decided to press to hear more and do it through written correspondence rather than discussing it face to face at this point. He wrote:

Dear Roberto,
Thank you for sharing with me your story about how the object came into your hands, and what it meant to you. I am eager to hear more. You are a good writer. And this is an interesting story and topic.

At the end of your account you say that three things were adding up to feel like a "conspiracy theory." You mentioned the following three things:

1. the dream your friend had about your dying
2. the dream you yourself had about dying
3. the object that was given to you

Can you tell me more about what you mean by conspiracy theory? Do you mean that something was being planned for you or that something was conspiring (making a conspiracy) about you or against you? Please say more. Also, please tell me more about why you gave up the object. You have said a lot so far about how it came into your hands, and what it made you think and feel. Now, please tell me a bit about why you gave it up, and when, and to whom.

I am looking forward to the next installment of your writing.

Mr. Harrison handed his letter to Roberto, in an envelope, in the hallway. Handing it to him, he said that he appreciated his writing and was asking to see more. Roberto took the envelope and moved into the milling students. It was a Friday. Monday morning he turned in what he called a second chapter. The ellipsis in the first paragraph is his.

Hollow Point chapter 2

I carried the bullet in between my thumb and index finger. Looking at the bronze lead head and the silver jacket. There was one thing I was wishing about that day where Floyd punched me in the face . . . I tell you what, it was the worst gruesome image I have ever pictured. That 9mm spear Luger hollow point bullet started looking very friendly that day. I was hoping that he would be in some big corner store hold up. Then the store clerk would pull the emergency silent alarm and then he would be in big trouble. Walks outside and fires a random few shots at the police crowd. Then the police would take action and fire their service pistols. I imagined that one bullet flying in the air, starting to split open and hitting him on the side of his stomach. The blood splatters on the wall. Floyd clutching onto his open wound. His blood stains the side walk. That was my wish for that day, but some things can't come true. I took the bullet and placed it on a bible and made a promise. I promised never to think of that again and that the 9mm would be used for justice and justice only. I thought [that] putting the bullet on the bible would purify the dreams and grudge. The bullet is nothing but a promise. The only way to use it for justice is to keep it away from the other piece that creates it into a killing tool.

"Bullets do not kill, Mr. Bond, it's the finger that pulls the trigger."

—*The Man with the Golden Gun*

Hopefully the act I did will change the way society is run, one at a time. I started it. Hopefully another is doing the same.

Roberto had said a lot, but he had made no mention of why he'd given the bullet to Tina. Mr. Harrison responded again in writing. It seemed that the most effective means to learn more would be to maintain the formality of the written correspondence:

Dear Roberto,

Thank you for this next chapter in your story. You are a talented writer—very descriptive. And you live your life with a strong sense of the importance of symbols and symbolic acts, which I think contributes to your good work as a writer.

In these pages, you tell about the Bible, and how you placed the object on the Bible and made a promise—a promise that you would never think certain thoughts again. You thought that by using the Bible you could purify the world of bad dreams and bad feelings (the grudge). You end these pages by stating your hope that your action might contribute to changing society for the better. I think this is a moving and powerful statement. You are recognizing that your small actions are actually big actions in that they can impact all of us—for the better. So, I have one more question for you to reflect upon.

The important act you refer to is the purification. This is indeed important. There is one more action I'd like to hear about: the action of giving up the object and giving it to another person.

Please write a bit about this as well, and reflect on these questions: After you purified the object, why did you hand it to someone else? What was the importance or symbolic importance of this action?

I look forward to at least one more entry in your story.

A day passed, then another. Mr. Harrison asked Roberto when he would be handing in the next installment. He hesitated. Mr. Harrison recalled what he'd said about Celeste, how she'd started to ask questions that were too personal. He might be pulling away, Mr. Harrison thought. So he reminded Roberto that while this wasn't a punishment, it was a requirement.

The next day Roberto submitted the next chapter, more hastily written, and without literary embellishments. As his chapter title confirmed, he was eager to end the correspondence:

Hollow Point—the final chapter
I do not remember what my intensions were on giving a twenty-four year old Caucasian woman a 9mm police issued round, but I was sure that it was something I should not have done. For some reason I remember watching Lethal Weapon and Martin Riggs (Mel Gibson) was with Roger Murtaugh (Danny Glover). Riggs was passing by for Christmas and gave Murtaugh a 9mm hollow point bullet because of the troubles he went through with him. For some reason I think I was copying that moment, because when I was punched Tina was there so mad, I just started crying. When I sucked it up and turned around I notice Tina was about to burst into tears. I tried manning up and all but a girl's tears can really convince a man to cry. Before the day we did our second town meeting Tina told em her wedding progress or something. I guess I just remembered that part of the movie and remembered that day. I notice even I had a 9mm bullet. I guess I wanted to have a movie moment.

Except Martin Riggs was suicidal, I was mad about hurting the person who hurt me 10 times worse. Funny I was reading *The Catcher in the Rye* and the main character said movies can really ruin someone. I can actually agree with that.

This is probably the one story with only 3 chapters that will never get published at all. But will be read by one man only.

In his concluding words he may be telling Mr. Harrison not to share this story—not with Tina, especially—or expressing a hope that he wouldn't. And he may have been anticipating that Mr. Harrison would want to hear still more, and so he was preemptively saying that here it ends, to be "read by one man only." An adolescent self-aggrandizement and some fatalism speak through.

Mr. Harrison did allow it to end there, the writing correspondence and the intervention. He was satisfied that Roberto had reflected on his motives and the principal's concerns and questions—though it would be hard to say that Roberto provided full clarity. Mr. Harrison was satisfied that Roberto was not at high risk of doing harm to himself or others. And the remainder of the school year went fine. He continued counseling sessions with Celeste when she returned. He began to look ahead to his senior year, to plan for college, and he was managing relationships in school without causing tears in the social fabric.

Roberto didn't let the story go, though. How could he? Narratives like this, the impressions are lasting. The impression of a fist on your face doesn't easily go away. Roberto carried the echo of the blow, and it continued to sound like a call for revenge.

"I WANT TO MURDER HIM!"

Any of us can recall the stories we've heard—or perhaps, tragically, experienced—of school shootings and teen suicides. A toxic mix of persecution and pain can indeed lead our young people to kill themselves and others.

Recall Roberto's vision, which he called a wish: "I carried the bullet in between my thumb and index finger. Looking at the bronze lead head and the silver jacket. There was one thing I was wishing about that day where Floyd punched me in the face . . ." Again, this ellipsis is his, then he writes, "I tell you what, it was the worst gruesome image I have ever pictured." He writes what comes next in fine detail: "I imagined that one bullet flying in the air, starting to split open and hitting him on the side of his stomach. The blood splatters on the wall. Floyd clutching onto his open wound. His blood stains the side walk."

A full year after Roberto wrote that passage for Mr. Harrison, he took an English class called "Writing from Within." And so Roberto found himself with another outlet from the revenge narrative that had been churning inside. He shared a story he'd written in the class with Celeste, who told him Mr. Harrison might be interested in reading it. He came to the principal's office one day at lunch and left it on the table.

Much of the story was the same, but Mr. Harrison was struck by something new. Two-thirds of the way through Roberto's retelling, his reliving of that day, he writes a new version of Floyd's destruction:

> I walked away preventing myself from getting into anymore trouble. *"I want to kill him! I want to murder him! I want him to bleed! I want to Arrrgh!"* That's all I could think about. I tried to avoid the satisfaction of my right fist to his left side of his jaw, dislocating his left side of his jaw. I would have sacrificed breaking three knuckles in the impact, but I would never have noticed it. Or the satisfaction of running him over with my father's white 1993 Toyota Camry at the speed of 90 miles per hour. I would see his skull smashing into the windshield, breaking into a thousand shards of red tinted glass, sprinkling into my face. His neck would twist and break due to the force of the impact. Then he would fly into the air and land eight feet in front of the car and tumble over. After that, he would lie on the ground, no movement at all, just sitting there with his head on the black tar.

Mr. Harrison didn't discuss it with him, since he knew Roberto was discussing it with Celeste. The next day, they crossed paths in the hallway.

To start conversation, Mr. Harrison asked what Roberto was planning to do over the coming summer. After a short exchange, Roberto asked what Mr. Harrison thought of the story.

Mr. Harrison thanked Roberto for sharing it and recollected how it had been meaningful to correspond with him last year on this same topic. He didn't remark that Roberto imagines Floyd dying in a new way in this story. Mr. Harrison didn't ask him where the bullet had gone, no longer in the story. But he did ask him how it felt to write about it again.

Roberto said it felt good to be getting it out there in class, hearing reactions from other students—because then you see that others can relate to it, and you don't feel so alone, "like you're not the only one." Mr. Harrison affirmed that it is important to share our stories with our peers.

"RESTRAINT OF REVENGE"

Roberto had given his story a new title: "Restraint of Revenge: Forcing Down Satisfaction." This account doesn't have the same musings on how his gesture will be a small one that changes society for the better, but Roberto does convey a sense of accomplishment in holding back and not acting on his destructive wish. He concludes this version of the story:

> My thoughts were lethal weapons, sharper than a double edge knife, yet harmless thoughts. It frustrated me that I did not hurt the boy in order to get rid of the craving of a clean punch left side of the forehead, but I did not ask for any trouble. He was not as articulate as I was, he had no self control. As much as I wanted to hurt him, I simply walked away in the sunlight as the eyes of people followed.

Roberto doesn't say what the eyes of others said to him, or what their voices said about him. It is likely that both inside and outside the school some of those eyes were asking, *Aren't you going to fight back?* Or calling him names like *punk* or *pussy*. Jeremiah—or the persona in his rhymes—wouldn't have tolerated walking away from the conflict. The gangster persona lives by a different code: "Bleeding dead meat . . . Put him down in the street." Boys like Jeremiah were certainly watching the day Roberto went down, but other eyes were watching too. They watched him walk around the corner—through their lunchtime loungings and conversations—back into the school, bleeding. Roberto came to the principal's office shaking.

Does it matter that the school he walked back to has a core value called "Commitment to Peace"? Not that he had this in mind as he walked inside; he was simply bewildered and afraid. But later that year his peers would nominate him to receive a Core Value Award for his self-restraint. And the following year he would rewrite the story's ending with self-congratulation for walking away.

What if he'd been in a different school? Would he have been able to take pride in not fighting back? Would he have been able to carry the story and ache for revenge for so long without finally making blood spill?

CIVILIZATION'S DISCONTENT

How different are Jeremiah and Roberto, the two boys whose writings have been explored in the last two chapters? There are notable contrasts. In the absence of stable family, inherited vocation, and traditional givers of meaning like the church, Jeremiah chooses an archetypical male posture to give his self-story some coherence. He becomes—outwardly—a conquering, consuming warrior. Ta-Nehisi Coates describes boys like Jeremiah from his childhood in Baltimore: "the young men who'd transmuted their fear into rage," who "walked the blocks of their neighborhood, loud and rude, because it was only though their loud rudeness that they might feel any sense of security and power."[3]

Roberto was different. He walked softly, unsure about where to find security and power. In fact, he knew some degree of basic security. He lived with his biological mother and father and had extended family members who cared for him. He had inherited a religious tradition, to which he felt allegiance. He went to school year after year with no incarceration interruptions. The police are not strangers putting bullets in his chest; the police are his brother-in-law giving him a bullet as a souvenir.

Jeremiah, confronted by both systemic and episodic violence, reciprocates the violence and aspires to gangsterhood and fame in his rhymes. He has settled his feet on that path and vision. Roberto, in contrast, struggles to settle on anything. While Jeremiah easily accesses masculine dominance narratives—get money, get sex, and get revenge if you get crossed—Roberto doesn't access any of this. Roberto just gets confused. Jeremiah simplifies, reductionist, in the mode of a brutal and consumerist society. In Jeremiah's rhymes human life, his own and that of others, has little to no meaning. Roberto is different. When it comes to making meaning, it's not that he has too little of it; he rather finds himself lost in an abundance of meaning.

Roberto's three chapters are penned by a young man who is sensitive to the potency of the symbols in his world. His writing offers insight into the many colliding and mixing symbolic worlds—enduring and fleeting—that young people travel through in America today. Roberto pulls from a variety of traditions in his effort to make sense of his life, to make a statement about his place and values, and to work through the trauma of being beaten, rejected, and defeated. We all need healthy ways to do this: to walk through, move past, or live with the pain in our lives, and we need symbolic paths fit for the journey.

Roberto calls on the Bible and the bullet. It's a classic pairing: the holy coupled to the hurtful, the blessed thing brought to the dark object. Classic symbolic symbiosis, but nevertheless a confusing tension, filled with questions as old as the first sacrifice: How to avenge and how to purify? How to tame the bloody vision? How to atone for sins imagined, and thus committed? How to rid oneself of the powerful object, or to use that object for good? And another question comes to mind, after reading the third and final chapter: How does Hollywood fit in? How does a melodrama-thick piece of movie-star denouement fit into this adolescent's puzzle of self, his striving for spiritual resolution, his need for coherence in his identity struggle?

Roberto carries a cross of civilization's discontent, the cross of symbolic confusion. He has been raised in a world of mixed metaphors, of interconnected and disconnected symbols, with no clear path to tell him: *This, Roberto, is how to purify; this is how to atone; this is how to become a man; this is where blood spills and we are made whole inside and out; this is when darkness comes, and here is how to transcend it; this is your duty, and this is not.* He was raised in a Catholic tradition, and sheltered—but in certain ways perhaps not sheltered enough. The symbolic coherence of his inherited stories—those of the church—had been punctured.

Certainly, some of Roberto's confusion is just symptomatic of adolescence. In teenage years, identity is explored; new clothes, myths, and prophecy are tried on. But part of it is a modern malaise animated by the question, usually unspoken: What to do with all that we have? All the things, information, symbols, choices, careers, places, roles? Intersecting in Roberto's three chapters are tropes and powerful objects from many different traditions, including deep-seated Christian traditions, age-old patriarchal postures, cliché "movie moments" that pretend catharsis, disaffected and misanthropic voices, images of bloodletting, dream-lives of self-destruction and torn flesh—and *more* torn flesh—and morality tales with unconvincing conclusions.

TOO MUCH MEANING

Roberto lives at a culmination, at the present moment in a long progression of cultural evolution. He also is living the good-faith struggle of the hypercivilized: his world is one of too much myth, meaning, image, and symbol. One might argue that Roberto needs a heaping dose of the deeply traditional—not the traditionally violent masculine identity strands that Jeremiah claimed, but a more unified and limited symbolic universe—and, yes, maybe even a real blood sacrifice, if that of the Eucharist has lost its hold on him.

Not to discount the power of this Christian ritual—by no means. Indeed, it is important to value those civilized spaces where people effectively work with signifiers of physical transformation, embodiments that are once, twice, or more removed from the material referent. Ritual symbolism allows us to live in language and art and to do without the truly violent. Eat and drink flesh and blood—symbolically, yes, if those objects you invest with the meaning truly hold it. But if they don't, there may be a need that goes unsatisfied.

And for many millennia in many places—and in many places now—the need for powerful symbols to help us see and transcend our pain is met when the red blood of animals and their white milk spills on simple rock altars or circles drawn on the ground, in small communities where ancestors emerge and guide the hand that holds the knife. Bloodletting is not the essential element here, and yet the most widely practiced religion of our time, Islam, still annually calls for the slit neck of the ram, as Abraham did. It is a representation of mythic sacrifice that is still, on one powerful level, not a representation, but real bloodletting. The point is that our symbols must be powerful, and they must be given space to breathe in an uncluttered cultural landscape, if they are to do their real work. Most youth today, by contrast, live in a very cluttered cultural landscape.

In his first chapter, Roberto mentions the driver education course he was taking. For many teens, earning the license to drive constitutes a major rite of passage into adulthood. Indeed, it has many of the essential ingredients of a traditional rite of passage. It is an elder, often a parent, who helps train the child. It is a physical training, an apprenticeship, and a handing over of tools and tasks. And the stakes are high—cars are heavy, move fast, can kill—and the reward is independence and the meaningful triumph that comes from the gradual transcendence of fear. It may be among our most meaningful and universal rites of passage in America. But is it adequate?

There are other rituals to mark maturation, certainly, but they are often jumbled. What most youth know today is a rites-of-passage cocktail, and it includes some religious elements, such as a first communion or bar mitzvah, and then there's driving, and prom, graduation and going to college, and drinking age. And there's sex, which happens in private, well before the public sanctioning and adult rite of marriage. Or it's sex that happens in a public gathering of adolescents, a real or social media gathering, where the community of adults has almost entirely abdicated its responsibility to guide and affirm.

A RETURN TO SOMETHING ELSE

Our country's ritual smorgasbord isn't nearly coherent enough to help adolescents adequately mark the transition into adulthood—and "adequately" means attending to and transcending the physical and spiritual crises, acknowledging the fear, accessing the hope, recognizing inheritance, giving new direction and new license in generally unified symbolic terms.

U.S. military training camps probably do this more effectively for young men—more coherently, and in a few weeks or months—than most other mainstream American institutions. And some of our more desperate young men will choose gang membership to provide them a rite of passage and sense of self; others will get the same through crime and doing time.

For young women there is that rite of passage that so many girls experience too early: becoming a mother. Of course, this passage has all the powerful essential elements of a traditional rite of passage: pain, transcendence, the physical embodiment of the journey, the object vessel of meaning, and the guidance of adult women, during birthing and then after, when suddenly the girl has become one of them.

What Roberto the teenager needs is not boot camp, and not fatherhood, not yet—but he does need physical and specific rites of passage to denote the frontier of manhood, and fewer roles to choose from, in a much less conflicted cultural landscape—perhaps even very little choice.

Roberto, like most people in Western society, lives outside the village, among the hypercivilized. But Roberto hasn't gone down the road to existentialist atheism, or sunk to postmodern nihilism; he's going down the path that good faith goes down when it's simply trying to maintain faith, to make meaning from too much meaning. His inherited religious symbols have been undermined, or augmented and confused. His instincts are unsure in their expression, without clear channels for exertion, and without clear means of repression or redirection either. It can be heard in his writing: the need to be taken by the hand, seated by a fire in the darkness and uncivilized a bit, made afraid but certain in his fear or rage, and given a clear light down the path to transcend it. But alas, the holy book and the mediocre movie climax are streams of equal meaning swirling in his mind. He needs a return to something else, perhaps some rite of passage through some actual wilderness that can mark his maturation and help clarify the adult world's expectations of him.

A physical and emotional testing, supported by adults and inherited tradition, are essential components to life in many indigenous communities. Parallel kinds of experiences are found in non-indigenous communities as well: in the rural United States, for instance, many families offer their children meaningful rites of passage into adulthood through mentorship into the powerful tools, emotional trials, and physical adventure of hunting. In other places, communal or familial rites of passage based in the natural world are rare, although there are profound "adventure learning" and self-discovery experiences that people with means can purchase for their children.

Roberto's school, for instance, is partnered with New York City Outward Bound, which takes kids to the woods each year to experience physical challenge, personal triumph, and a sense of new belonging to a group. It is a fine experience, but it only scratches the surface of the deeply transformative Outward Bound journeys that families with means can buy for their children—or themselves—at a price tag of many thousands of dollars.

During such adventures, the young person spends a week, or weeks, in the hands of expert guides, moving through conditions of challenge appropriately calibrated to his or her developmental and physical capacities, in which group dynamics and solo journeys into physical and spiritual solitude offer great new meanings and the sense of newfound self. It is much the same thing that can be seen in some traditional societies that still send their young men into the bush for days, to return with new status, rights, and expectations placed on them.

During the same time Mr. Harrison was reading Roberto's writing, another student handed Mr. Harrison some pages he'd written. This boy was new to the school, a recent transfer in his senior year. He came from a white family of significant material stability compared to most of the other boys in the school. It was his college application essay he handed Mr. Harrison, his personal statement, and it spoke of a transformation.

It begins with a circle of fire, a mountaintop, and a small group of people living in close quarters. He tells of how he was sent on two great journeys by his family, on the heels of a difficult spiraling time: first a journey into the wilderness of Maine, and then into the Rocky Mountains. These journeys helped him run from himself, through himself, and toward his next self. He recounts a heart-tearing sprint down a mountain, his feet trying to catch up to where his inner voice was charging. He relives why he ran so fast and hard: because he was running from a past of melancholy, passivity, and failure, running toward a refusal to deny any longer his potential. His essay pulses with the forceful sense of self that his adventure in the wilderness had helped him discover.

His parents did right in providing him this journey, a simplification and paring away, a confrontation with simple and strong life forces. Like him, Roberto and Jeremiah and all young people need simple, powerful—and humane—identity markers to help them chart their ways.

THE DIS-ORDERED WORLD

One should not idealize village life. Life is not simple anywhere or in any era, and souls struggle and souls are nourished in the circled huts of Senegal just as they are on the Left Bank of Paris. Indeed, before she departed for her native home, Celeste—the social worker who worked with Roberto—discussed with Mr. Harrison her return to the remote village where she would help bury her father according to a traditional culture's long-standing ways. Had she not left in her childhood, she is certain she would now be dead, and before death she'd have been a girl with nary a drop of agency in her world.

Every village or every human tradition cannot be categorically revered, but our work with young people—including in schools—must allow certain traditional societal traits their weight and place and due. "Village" is a convenient metaphor for our human past in small groups. There is wisdom in the cliché, "It takes a village to raise a child." But in fact our species spent more of our evolutionary journey in smaller hunting-and-gathering kinship bands. In these foraging bands, people didn't sit still for too long, didn't have much stuff, and there wasn't exactly a "village." But the village metaphor recalls a past that most people can sense, a traditional tight-knit community form we can culturally recall—and one that deserves our attention.

Our brains as they are now were built in small community groups, very small intergenerational societies, with simple divisions of labor, oriented to common tasks, largely egalitarian though hierarchical by merit and age, with a shared past and shared spiritual and material goals—common endeavors born of common earth, wind, and circumstance.

And now, very suddenly in evolutionary time, we have built cities and suburbs, and our virtual worlds, and our networks for the rapid global trading of goods and ideas and selves. These new circumstances propel our human being down vastly different pathways and highways than what people's minds and spirits were built to travel. It's not traditional, normal, or ordinary to the species, and this is a wellspring of malaise.

Why have people left small communities behind? Why do we seem to have only the individual self or the anonymous mass, and so little in between? Climate activist and scholar Bill McKibben argues that the deconstruction of traditional human community is of a piece with our recent destruction of the earth: "Access to endless amounts of cheap energy made us rich, and wrecked our climate, *and it also made us the first people on earth who had no practical need of our neighbors.*"[4] Or as David Owen puts it in *Green Metropolis*, "before cars, people lived close to other people to survive; with cars, proximity became less important—indeed, it became undesirable."[5]

So our independence and hyperindividualism came quickly into our lives over the past two hundred years fueled by carbon extracted from the ground.

But the journey began much earlier, and much positive has come with the negative. Bill McKibben offers a synopsis:

> The story of the last five hundred years is the story of continual emancipation. The people of the modern world have freed themselves from innumerable oppressions: absolute monarchy, feudalism, serfdom, slavery. Five hundred years ago, if you were a European, you most likely rested in the bosom of the church, as a small part of the Great Chain of Being that was medieval Christendom. You were born in a village, and there you would likely spend the rest of your life; the world outside was unsafe, the lair of bandits and wild animals. . . . Your spouse would come from a small pool of eligible partners, and once you married you would in all likelihood stay that way. You inherited your profession from your parents and passed it down to your children.
>
> Many factors dissolved this ordered world. Most notably, the new religious idea of the Protestant movement—that each of us was responsible for his or her own salvation—began to erode the old idea of one true church. The work begun by the Reformation was finished by fossil fuel, which freed farmers from the land, liberated us from days of manual labor, and granted us a mobility that expanded human horizons. . . .
>
> All of these liberations have brought benefit, often great benefit: they have helped produce the ideas we hold dearest, such as democracy; they have helped spur the civil rights and women's revolutions; and they have made us much, much richer. But most of them also carried costs, sometimes harder for us to see. We surrendered a fixed identity—a community, an extended family, deep and comforting roots—for, quite literally, the chance to "make something of ourselves."[6]

And so we raise today's individuals, like Roberto, unmoored from fixed identities, children on their own trying to make something of themselves. Parents and teachers ask children at young ages: *So what do you want to be?*

To be? That's a big question. Existential freedom such as this isn't an easy weight to carry. But what are the right kinds of constraints, parameters, boundaries, bonds? It is important to have boundaries and bonds.

"LIVING THE DREAM"

Clear statements of values offer one way to provide boundaries. Roberto's peers nominated him for a Core Value Award, honoring his Commitment to Peace, one of the school's seven core values. He was nominated for the restraint he showed when faced with the allure of revenge. It made an impression on his fellow students. As it turned out, the adults at the school didn't allow Roberto to receive a Core Value Award that semester, because holding him accountable for a misstep he'd made in another area meant he wasn't eligible for it. But this is another clear and appropriate boundary for an adult community to offer a young person.

Roberto's small school community was able to give him something of the village it takes to raise a child: boundaries, bonds, and the valuing of his story. Picture him in his senior year, the year after the bullet, in his English class, writing from within: he is in dialogue, in a small circle, in a small class, in a small school, recasting his painful memory and revenge fantasy in a public and creative medium—instead of living this wish as a hurtful act, or destructive melancholy inaction. And he has peers in this community who tell him that they empathize.

He has a teacher who encourages him to resurrect his past, to know and speak it. He has a social worker, principal, advisor, and other adults who care about his inner life, and he knows it. His super-ego has its real-people referents—people who tell him what behavior is valued and what behavior is not OK—and he is learning to forecast the potential consequences of his actions and to adjust his impulses accordingly.

During that semester of his senior year when Roberto was writing from within, Mr. Harrison ran into Roberto on his way home. Both were heading by subway train to one of New York City's outer boroughs. The timing of their commutes had never aligned in this way before. They sat on the warm plastic bench in the subway car, across from a placard that told them to be vigilant: "If you see something, say something." Other signs—advertisements—promised cheap salvation through plastic surgery, lawsuits, and alcohol. Happily, they had each other to talk to.

The train was stopped, waiting for passengers at the beginning of the route. They talked of quotidian things: Roberto's classes, his advisory group, his thoughts on college next year, the driver education classes he was taking. He told Mr. Harrison he'd failed in his first attempt at the road test, and that his dad had once promised him a car if he achieved a certain GPA, but now the father's expectation was that he just get into college.

The train jolted and began to pull them across the city. Along the way, Mr. Harrison asked about Roberto's friendships. Roberto described how he found it hard to meet girls in the city or to get to know them. They talked of his sister and her boyfriend, the one who'd given him the bullet. They'd had a child, and Roberto described his pledge to be the best uncle the child ever had. "Well, I'm the only uncle," he said, "but I'll be the very best one ever." He asked Mr. Harrison about his son, just a year old.

Mr. Harrison shared a bit about his wife and child. He asked about Roberto's parents and how they'd met. Roberto told a story of his father's friend, who met a girl who had a sister, and then came a magical double date, and then it was happily ever after. He easily recounted the story as if he'd heard it told many times. It was one of those tales of how accident or deity suddenly smiles on people and leads them to love.

Reciprocating somewhere under the water between Manhattan and Brooklyn, Roberto asked Mr. Harrison how he and his wife had met. Mr.

Harrison told him the story, noting how they were nearing an anniversary and how he was planning to bring his wife a gift. Roberto said, "Wow, man. You're really living the dream."

LOVE: THE BASIC WISH

What dream was Roberto talking about? What hope or wish?

Roberto was affirming the basic power of a simple dream, a traditional dream: falling in love, getting married, having a child, and celebrating an anniversary. Perhaps he imagined Mr. Harrison walking into his house with an anniversary bouquet of roses, or sending his wife a box of chocolates and a poem. Whatever symbol of love he saw being offered—perhaps with a hand behind the back, or on a knee, or some other gesture of chivalry or devotion—Roberto was affirming the importance of simple things, of love as the dream.

Maybe Roberto was not so confused after all. Love is the simple and basic wish. Jeremiah's girlfriend was affirming the same in her letter to him, the gangster boyfriend she was trying to love into the home from the street. She was also envisioning a future when they would have and hold a child, recalling those simple times they sat and just talked. Roberto was voicing the same simple hope, the light at the end of his tunnel. He was bringing it back to basics, simple bonds and boundaries. Soon, Mr. Harrison and Roberto would say goodbye, each leaving the common train to transfer to another, and Mr. Harrison walking with doubled haste down the tunnel connecting to the next train home.

QUESTIONS FOR REFLECTION AND DISCUSSION

1. What aspects of Roberto's writing struck you as interesting or significant, and why?
2. Roberto experienced violence during lunchtime at school. What do you think of how the principal and the school handled the incident and its aftermath?
3. What rites of passage help young people in your community mark the transition from adolescence into adulthood? Are they healthy, positive experiences?
4. In your community, how do religion, pop culture, school life, and other influences intersect to shape the identity journey of young adults?

Chapter Four

SEETHE

I became, during my fourteenth year, for the first time in my life, afraid—afraid of the evil within me and the evil without.

—James Baldwin[1]

What drew me in at fourteen years old was I was searching for identity, community and purpose.

—Christian Picciolini, former neo-Nazi[2]

Adolescents, like all of us, have simple needs and hopes at the core. They express themselves in various ways, as diverse as the human family is diverse. We can discover how these needs and hopes form a special constellation for each child by carefully listening to each child's voice. To most of them we only need extend the right kind of invitation to begin to hear their stories.

But what about the children who are less expressive, who don't write poems, who don't cut, who don't harm others, who say little, who don't or won't write? What about the kids who instead seethe quietly, without appropriate paths to express their pain and direct their energies? Some of these children who seethe quietly also seethe darkly, contemplating final solutions.

What can we learn from young people in crises so deep that they cultivate fantasies of homicide—and sometimes perpetrate the violence on their communities? As it turns out, much can be learned about adolescent normalcy from an adolescent in crisis. The typical identity needs and longings of most adolescents are illuminated when we look closely at children experiencing more extreme identity troubles.

In a time of identity confusion, there is good to come from simplification, narrowing parameters, and focusing on what is most important. We hear this from Jeremiah and his girlfriend, and from Roberto. Simple values and wishes can provide us what we need, or guide us to it.

But reduction and narrowing also comes with danger. Simplification of worldview can bleed into oversimplification, insularity, and stereotype. This enables the dehumanization of others, which can easily enable violence. Violence can then become a means to affirm your own humanity, or at least know your power, secure your place, and hear your name. And it sounds like hate. "Hate gives identity," writes Ta-Nehisi Coates; "The nigger, the fag, the bitch illuminate the border, illuminate what we ostensibly are not."[3]

We want our children to know themselves as powerful and to sense the borders of a secure identity. But if we allow them to wall in or narrow too much their identities and their understandings of others, there is risk of hatefulness. The means we use to help them know their goodness and feel their force matters greatly.

CLEAR AND SIMPLE DICTATES

In *Letters to a Young Muslim*, Omar Ghobash writes to his son, Saif—and to all young Muslims and young people. His second letter is called "The Gray Area," in which he catalogs many of the identity challenges his adolescent son is facing. They are challenges that confront most young people today, no matter the religion or place.

The father is speaking here of challenges born of overexposure to unsettling and unending stimuli: the media coverage of everything, everywhere, from the mundane to the miraculous; the constant barrage of violent images, sexual images, irreverent and holy images; the confusion of remembrance and forgetting that is history, ever contested; the battle between competing ideologies for the right to be Truth; the varying demands and values of home, school, street, and wider world. The father asks, "Where is the meaning and purpose in all of this?"[4] He empathically understands that, when faced with vast complexity and confusion, there arises a need for simplicity of purpose and meaning. Ghobash describes the "very simple" and narrow ideas that can thus hold strong allure for a young person seeking an end to this confusion.[5] These ideas come packaged in easy categories: us/them, good/evil, right/wrong, pure/impure, clean/dirty, human/animal.

The father acknowledges the violence of the world in which the identity strivings of his son unfold. He validates the outrage his son must feel at the brutality he sees wielded over his near and distant kin, his fellow Muslims, all over the world. He notes the powerful allure of online and in-person purveyors of pat answers to complex questions.

The father understands how a child could be drawn to those who righteously claim to offer the one and only way to manhood, holiness, or salvation. He remarks on the power of what they profess: "The path is clear, the language is straightforward and simple. When all the clutter of modern life is removed, the path opens up before you toward meaning and purpose."[6]

Yes, young people seek and need big ideas, greater meaning, and purpose. And as Erik Erikson remarked in the unstable post–World War II era, adults in times of great change can appear to youth as if they've abdicated their responsibility to make greater meaning, acting instead like kids obsessed with petty concerns. Ghobash acknowledges how powerless and out-of-touch the adults of this world can appear to a young person today:

> You believe that your parents do not understand the issues you face. They live in a different world. They are content with the mind-numbing and backbreaking work they do. They are isolated and powerless in the face of technologies and economic forces. . . . You are embarrassed. . . . They do not have any convincing answers to your questions. In fact, not only are they not living up to the clear and simple dictates of Islam, but they are also dinosaurs who have no role in this life. You love them, but they are peripheral in the great battle of Good against Evil.[7]

Soon the empathic father voice imagines the dreaded conclusion some youth may reach, that the world is polluted and needs cleansing—and then violence becomes the simple solution.

"NOT UNLIKE THE COLUMBINE KILLERS"

Lawrence Friedman, an Erik Erikson biographer, noted how it was just five years after Erikson passed away that two young men went on a rampage inside Columbine High School in Littleton, Colorado. The two boys assassinated their peers and then killed themselves. Friedman asserts there was a "deep inner sense of emptiness and inadequacy" in the boys.[8] He notes the relevance of Erikson's observations about how youth, in their search for power and certainty, can be drawn to rigid and totalizing worldviews. Such was "Hitler's appeal to unsteady German youth" in the last century:

> Promoting himself as the head of a juvenile delinquent gang, Hitler told German youngsters (who were not unlike the Columbine killers) to bypass their parents and local community standards of respectability and to gain identity negatively—by assaulting Jews, homosexuals, gypsies, the handicapped, Communists, and other "undesirables." One learned what one was and gained a sense of destiny by turning with Hitler against these enemies of the *volk*.[9]

Viewing others as not "us," not good, not clean, is a kind of other-ing typical of adolescence. We often call it bullying, and it includes emotional and actual violence. Adolescents are good at this kind of thing, and they will tend toward it more, and with higher stakes attached, in times when the adult world around them struggles with great uncertainty and upheaval. Such is our time in many places, including many of our American cities, towns, and rural communities. War and climate change unsettle us. Social bonds are undone by the corrosion of depression and addiction. State violence kills many and incarcerates millions, crippling families for generations as institutionalized oppression has done for hundreds of years.

What Erikson saw in the mid-twentieth century is true today: "the mechanisms of adjustment which once made for psychosocial evolution, tribal integration, and national or class coherence are at loose ends."[10] Young people, in times of social disintegration and incoherence, will find it hard to choose the empathic and nonviolent path toward knowing who they are and how to be. "[M]any a sick or desperate late adolescent," concludes Erikson, "would rather be nobody or somebody totally bad or, indeed, dead—and this by free choice—than be not-quite-somebody."[11] As Ghobash does in his letter to his son, it is important that adults today honor this potential in our youth, and work hard in times of upheaval to help young people choose paths that don't end in feeling like a not-quite-somebody who then seeks selfhood through badness.

NOVEMBER SOULS

At the opening of Herman Melville's *Moby Dick*, the protagonist, a young man, takes flight. His name is Ishmael and he has death on his brain, aggression in his veins, and "a damp, drizzly November" in his soul. He is trying to cope, to stave off the darkness. Ishmael decides to take himself to sea rather than take up "pistol and ball." Ishmael also tells us in these opening lines that, at some time or another, most other men "cherish very nearly the same feelings."[12] Is he right about this? How common are the feelings that might compel a youth to pick up a gun?

Homicidal and suicidal talk is certainly not uncommon among young people. We have heard it in the writing of the young people shared in earlier chapters. We hear it in the hallways and in social media forums. Sometimes it's hyperbole and playful: "Oh my God, I almost died!" she says. Sometimes it's rage: "I'm going to fucking kill him," he says, punching the wall, breaking a bone. Sometimes it's carelessly mean: "Hey, go kill yourself," says a boy, insincerely, to a girl in the hall who becomes sincerely wounded.

Many young people have suicidal thoughts, if not suicidal plans. When "what I am" is difficult to know, "what if I wasn't?" can be easy to wonder. But it's hard to know if Ishmael is right. Most young people never find themselves at or close to the precipice of killing others or themselves. But it's not always easy to gauge the depth of the aggression a person is feeling, the scale of the fantasy, the details of the plans.

We do know that when it comes to dying a violent death in America, young men are often involved. These deaths happen in different ways, for various reasons. Environment, race, and class can be important factors. In most urban settings, almost every educator knows a boy—a black or Latino boy—who has taken a bullet and died. In most rural settings, in New England, for instance, almost everyone knows a boy who has hit a tree going too fast on a four-wheeler, or been thrown from the snow machine, or been killed in a car wreck. These are two very different contexts for growing up, for living and dying—and for teaching.

Wherever we work, though, we can be sure that some young people, like Ishmael, carry a grim November in their soul. And people who work in schools, especially public schools, know that if there is a suicidal or homicidal adolescent in the community, they are probably in routine and familiar contact with this young person. This is a privileged position. It is a privilege to do the important work of helping kids channel pain and aggression into hopeful, rather than harmful, designs.

TWO BOYS DETAINED

It was a damp November New England night when Mrs. Preston, a high school principal, got the call from her superintendent. It was a Sunday, and the superintendent had just been contacted by police, informed of the threat, and told that two boys would not be in school the following day.

The school's crisis response team met early before the start of school on Monday. The police had by then informed the superintendent that certain media outlets were already aware of what was going on: there was a plan, two boys were detained, and some bladed weapons had been confiscated. And this is the extent of the general public knowledge of the incident to this day.

As of 7:00 a.m., however, the superintendent hadn't canceled school, and wouldn't, for the police had said there was no imminent danger. The school had not yet contacted families or informed other school personnel, but within the next forty-five minutes, after students were settled into morning advisory class, a phone message was sent to families and the students and faculty were gathered together. It was a grade 7 to grade 12 school of about 450 students. Mrs. Preston and her team divided up to create smaller gatherings, high school in the auditorium with the associate principal, younger grades in the gym with Mrs. Preston. The phone message home and the words to students and faculty were shaped by the same talking points:

- There was information received over the weekend that two high school students were planning violence toward other members of the community.
- Authorities are in control. We are working closely with our police department and taking all precautions to keep students and all school community members safe. You are safe.
- We do not know whom exactly their plans are targeting. The police department is handling the investigation at this point.
- The police have issued a no trespass order so that we will not see the two students on school grounds while investigations are underway.
- A phone message has just gone out to all of your families.
- To respect the privacy rights of minors involved, this is the limit of the information we have to share at this point.
- Tomorrow, Tuesday, is a national holiday, and there is no school. We will start the day on Wednesday, after advisory, by gathering again in these assemblies so we can update you on how things are going.
- If you want/need to share your feelings on this matter, please see your school counselor or one of the principals to share your thoughts.
- Teachers, as we transition back to classes, if you perceive students needing to continue any aspect of this discussion, you are welcome to conduct it. You can write down notes and any questions or topics you don't feel prepared to address. You can also call to request that one of the principals or counselors join you.

Of course, students started crowding into the counselors' offices. Families started calling and arriving at school. The phone lines were clogged. Parents wanted more information than could be given. Indeed, few of the school leaders, based on what information they had, could even know the true extent of the threat.

Fear was in the air, and this was the hardest part of the day for everyone. Many people imagined the worst or believed the threat still lingered. About one-third of the students went home. From Mrs. Preston's vantage point, reflecting on it afterwards, the students most upset that Monday may have been those closest to the threat, closest to the boys. As Mrs. Preston would soon find out, some of the friends even had some knowledge of the boys' dark visions.

COMMUNITY DISRUPTED

This wasn't a case like Columbine, where roles of bully and bullied became long fixed, generating the dangerous dynamic of persecution, dehumanization, and vengeful fantasy. As far as the school was able to learn, the boys involved in this case were not bullied. They had friends across different social groups. To the extent that some of their plans were discussed among peers, those who heard or joined the conversation generally thought it part of some dark play.

The prevalence of homicidal and suicidal talk among adolescents—and within the broader popular culture—makes it possible that talk of violent plans could appear to peers as somewhat normal teenage exaggeration. But that doesn't negate this as one of the more troubling aspects of the incident for Mrs. Preston and colleagues: some kids knew something, and didn't tell.

The general feeling of safety in the school community was disrupted that morning. Mrs. Preston brought the faculty together after school. She shared the names of the two students. There were some gasps of surprise.

Mrs. Preston shared again what information she could. One of the school counselors reminded the faculty that there would be questions they may not ever be able to answer, that the interior life of another person can be difficult to fully understand. They reminded the faculty of the plan to bring the school together again on Wednesday morning. They invited those who wanted to talk more to stick around.

Afterward, a small group of faculty moved to a classroom. The director of guidance suggested they offer the parent community an opportunity to meet tomorrow. It was a good idea. Phone calls they'd not been able to answer were piled up in voicemail boxes. They would return the calls, but most parents needed the opportunity to discuss this incident face to face. There was no school the next day, but they hosted an open community meeting in the evening.

One parent, whose child had once been at school in another state when there was a shooting, described that incident as "the most chaotic situation" and said that what she'd experienced in this case "was one thousand times better." She said, "My son never once felt threat or fear." There wasn't panic, she noted. It was just "really heavy."

Mrs. Preston and colleagues assured the parents in the room that, with the two boys now in custody and hopefully getting the kind of care that they needed, the focus would be on the rest of the school's children and what they were feeling and needing.

Of course, the wellness of the faculty was a concern too. Adults can't care for kids if they don't care for themselves. So Mrs. Preston was glad to see by e-mail later that morning that a colleague with a degree in mental health had taken the initiative to offer faculty and staff an open room for discussing their own feelings after school. Several people attended, including Mrs. Preston. The adults were slowly moving out of crisis response into reflection.

That evening, at home, after her children were asleep, Mrs. Preston spent some time putting her kids' picture books and toys back on the shelves in the living room. It was a good, simple, repetitive task—and it was then that the sadness struck, and the feelings of guilt and failure.

FEELING SAFE IS NOT THE SAME AS BEING SAFE

Mrs. Preston spent hours that night online researching the work of Dr. Stuart Twemlow, a man whose work in schools is connected to crisis response, violence prevention, and the psychology of aggression. In one online interview, Twemlow notes that less than 1 percent of humans are psychopathic, which is a small number, a rarity. But, Mrs. Preston realized, that means in a school of several hundred there are going to be a few such people.

Mrs. Preston needed help to think it through further. She'd once met Dr. Twemlow at a conference. She resolved to reach out to him in the morning, a resolution that brought some certainty and allowed her to sleep for a few hours.

It was quiet at school on Wednesday, everyone seeking the security of routine. There was a pause in the typical misbehaviors and occasional trips to the principal's office. Mrs. Preston took some time to print and start reading two of Twemlow's papers: "Assessing Adolescents Who Threaten Homicide in Schools" and "A Crucible for Murder: The Social Context of Violent Children and Adolescents."

Twemlow is an analyst and an academic, but the ivory tower and the private office have doors at street level. Twemlow's feet are often in schools—of all types—and much of his research is available free online. Mrs. Preston dug up an e-mail conversation they'd had several years ago, and sent him a note to ask if he would join her and colleagues in a phone discussion. Within a day they were in correspondence and planning the conversation. Mrs. Preston e-mailed Twemlow on the day of the call with a list of observations and questions. She wrote:

> It seems to me that, in our case, we have two students whose violent fantasies were not born of the typical bully-victim-bystander dynamic in schools. I can't speak here to what the two accused students may have known in other social contexts. However, the role of the school bystander is indeed significant here. It seems to me that bystanders may have unwittingly nourished the violent fantasy. You note that "With dangerous children, the peer group has a developmentally exaggerated influence."[13] Can you share with us some more of your thoughts on this?
>
> You note that there are schools where the inner life of the child is viewed in mechanistic fashion: "A child who feels managed may cease to function as a whole human being in such a system, instead functioning like a collection of behaviors."[14] Can you talk about ways that this can be made better or worse in school classrooms? How can we help students feel like whole beings?
>
> After such frightening events in schools, you say that it is possible for "both students and teachers to continue to feel unsafe." This can happen when "the student making the threat did not return to school, remaining a mysterious 'presence' in the school because of fantasy and rumor."[15] We may face a

similar situation—indeed may be facing it now. How can a school deal with this?

Can you describe the different types of bystanders and discuss how schools can nurture the "altruistic bystander?"

What other questions should we be asking ourselves in the wake of this kind of threat event?

On Monday afternoon, Mrs. Preston and colleagues met in a conference room, Twemlow on speakerphone. Mrs. Preston was feeling nervous, both for the content of the conversation—new ground for her as a school leader—and because of Twemlow's stature. He works with the FBI and the Secret Service, and he travels the world helping to address issues of violence in schools. But he is also a caring man, generously giving his time that afternoon, and someone whose experience quickly helped him understand what questions and guidance the faculty needed to hear.

After fifteen minutes of discussion between Twemlow and Mrs. Preston, the first teacher to speak described his own feelings of pain, doubt, and failure. He wondered aloud why they hadn't seen it coming, what they'd done wrong, why other kids hadn't said anything, and what signs were missed.

With this comment, there was a release in the room, a relief, as if feelings the teachers were holding in had finally been named. Twemlow responded, and others joined in. They talked a full hour. By the time they said goodbye, the conversation had helped the educators put the incident into broader perspectives: historical, cultural, developmental. These are some of the notes Mrs. Preston gathered and then shared in a memo to the rest of the faculty:

- It was helpful to be reminded that the threat we felt/feel here at our school is something not uncommon for people/institutions working with adolescents. School shootings are, however, rare.
- Adolescents, more than adults or young children, are developmentally more likely to commit crimes and to develop suicidal and homicidal ideation.
- Very few people ever kill themselves or others, and it is difficult to know who is on such a path. Our intuition can be as good a guide as any objective data. Our climate in the school is key to allowing us to know students well enough for our intuition to work effectively.
- Feeling safe and being safe are very different states of being. We live in a dangerous, unsafe world. Crossing the street is unsafe. Driving a car is unsafe. But we typically feel safe in those situations. The key for us in our current school situation here is to recognize that some of us were made to feel unsafe, and to reflect on why this is, how it came about, and what we can do to re-establish a sense of safety.

- It was helpful to have teachers share the sense of sadness, shock, guilt that we can feel in the wake of such incidents. It was helpful to hear Stuart remind us that we don't and can't have all the answers; that we are not a bad school or a failure for having experienced this disruption to our community.
- We discussed how bullying is a process, not a person. There are flexible roles: the bully, the victim, the bystander. These are roles we all commonly play, moving in and out of them from situation to situation. The problem is when people become fixed in a role, for example, as a victim. This becoming fixed can be dangerous when it leads to a sense of total victimhood, of the world as being unjust and without value. If the world is without value, then one's own life and the lives of others can be seen to be without value.
- How to respond in this situation? For now, let things settle. Then, Stuart recommends, convene focus groups like this one, a month or two from now, when normalcy has been re-established. These groups should be open to all stakeholders—parents, custodians, students, etc.—and allow us to continue to reflect on why/how our sense of safety was disrupted and how we can continue to build a cohesive and safe community in the future.

After a year away from the school, in different settings, each boy returned. There were separate and formidable restorative justice processes for each boy. The boys seemed to do well in their remaining years, outwardly at least.

But what Mrs. Preston and colleagues truly knew about either boy's individual inner life was limited. And what details can be shared about minors in such situations is also limited. But we can focus on what educators can learn from such incidents. What can the school crisis—an exceptional disruption to a sense of safety—teach us about normal, day-to-day schooling? More specifically, what can research about violent adolescents teach us about all students?

DAILY VIOLENCE

Crime, Twemlow writes, "is primarily developmental," and "most crime, especially violent crime, is committed by adolescents."[16] What are the implications of this? Is criminality a developmental stage? Exactly what kind of criminality, aggression, or violence is developmentally typical of the adolescents educators work with?

In the months after the November incident at his school, several boys began to appear in Mrs. Preston's mind's eye and worry her. And there was one boy in particular. Mrs. Preston thought of him and the large group of friends and peers with whom he interacted each day, ninth-grade boys. Mrs. Preston began to see the violence more clearly.

"Bullying is violent," says Twemlow, "but does not consist merely of fighting"; it "usually involves a stronger, more dominant personality who repetitively coerces a weaker, more submissive personality." In bullying, the injuries are rarely physical: "The major injury is emotional humiliation."[17]

Mrs. Preston began using Twemlow's descriptions of bullying in conversations with this boy and his peers, who seemed to be stuck in a never-ending cycle of joking and shaming, teasing and taunting. She started pulling them into her office during lunch, or from the hallways before school. They sat in small groups, pairs, or sometimes it would be just the principal and one boy. They discussed the trio of roles—bully, victim, bystander—and how the roles can be interchangeable.

In one discussion with four of the boys, Mrs. Preston asked which role each of them seems to play most often. They agreed that the other boy is most frequently the victim. They did well at this level of self-reflection. They were a bit more puzzled by the idea of transference, the notion that bullies and bystanders may often project onto the victim, in Twemlow's words, certain "unwanted, usually frightening and disavowed parts of his or her own self" and then work to destroy that projection of the self.[18]

Mrs. Preston told the boys that if their problematic behavior continued, there would be, as there had been in the past, traditional interventions and consequences, like harassment reports, suspensions, and parent meetings. But she also told them that the real power to address this situation—a dynamic they knew was undignified and hurtful—was within each of them.

Sometimes, with more knowledge of how the dynamic works, young people can increase their capacity to choose to act contrary to their custom. And what had become customary for these boys needed to stop. "When these roles become fixed," writes Twemlow, "serious violence can be imminent."[19]

Mrs. Preston didn't fully explore this last idea with them. They didn't pursue how a special danger emerges when someone becomes too stuck in the victim role. In the shadow of the school's November threat incident, she didn't want to discuss the potential for an "avenging victim" to do serious violence to others, or to himself. They were not far enough away from November for it to be helpful to invite visions of bloodshed. So they didn't pursue where the path they were on might ultimately lead, and Mrs. Preston didn't tell them that she was pulling quotes from an essay about kids who kill other kids.

SERIOUS VIOLENCE

Twemlow articulates "three principles" that "underlie a psychoanalytic understanding of a threat":

1. Homicidal aggression is a drive, derived from interpersonal experience as well as genetic factors.
2. Aggressive impulses have control, modulation, and direction components, which can be altered by environmental influences.
3. Family and social control mechanisms can limit damage, irrespective of individual psychopathology.[20]

In his own work to limit the harmful expressions of the adolescent aggressive drive, Twemlow has become an advocate for the martial arts, developing programs in schools that explicitly cultivate "gentle warriors." The term is a good one, for it acknowledges that war-making muscle is there in our young people, while asserting that gentleness, in fact, is a force that our war-making bodies can exert.

Despite this reference here to war-making, it must be remembered that serious violence by children in schools is rare, and the sociopath and psychopath are few in number. In its 2016 "School Violence Fact Sheet," the Centers for Disease Control reports that less than 2.6 percent of all youth homicides occur at school, a statistic that has been "relatively stable for the past decade."[21] It is fair to assume that most schools, in collaboration with families and other stakeholders, do a good job of recognizing kids with strong potential for severe violence, and that alternative settings are typically found for these people to get care and education. One can furthermore hope—though it's certainly not always the case—that where these kids end up is not an incarceration situation where a mental illness or emotional distress goes untreated or gets worse.

As Twemlow notes, seriously violent young people are the exception to the rule, and so we should treat them differently and offer them different supports. But what do we do with the aggression more typical of normal adolescents? First, we must acknowledge that it's there: aggression is a drive, born of our bodies and in response to our environment. Second, we must work to shape its direction and limit the damage it might do.

THE W/HOLE CHILD

Teaching "the whole child" is a compelling notion. In her essay "What Does It Mean to Educate the Whole Child?" Nel Noddings speaks not only of the whole child but of whole people—whole teachers and whole communities:

We will not find the solution to problems of violence, alienation, ignorance, and unhappiness in increasing our security apparatus, imposing more tests, punishing schools for their failure to produce 100 percent proficiency. . . . Instead, we must allow teachers and students to interact as whole persons, and we must develop policies that treat the school as a whole community. The future of both our children and our democracy depend on our moving in this direction.[22]

At the high school level, one of the barriers that keeps our country from moving in this direction is the belief that elementary school teachers are experts in child development and high school teachers are experts only in their content areas—while middle school educators are some kind of hybrid. But high school teachers need to honor the whole child, too. And we need to understand that the whole child also has *holes*: longings, absences, troubles.

In 2014, Mrs. Preston's school hosted a community viewing of *The Hungry Heart* (2013), a documentary about people, many of them teens, who are addicted to opiates.[23] One couple in the film is in their early twenties. They sit on a couch, their infant with them, held in the arms of their thin bodies. Their cheekbones are in high relief, their eyes recessed. They are working on recovery. They talk of once feeling whole. They shake their heads in reverence of the awesome experience that was their first opiate high, that total feeling of totality, of completeness.

Watching this film, a refrain emerges: "For the first time, I felt whole." Or, "It filled a hole inside me." And it's not just people from difficult socioeconomic circumstances who become addicted to such drugs and such feelings. All people are in some way vulnerable because everyone has holes that ache to be filled.

Educators don't always want to talk about these matters. Twemlow remarks that teachers sometimes avoid such topics because we can be "overly optimistic and positive thinking, afraid of litigation from parents, and have narcissistic needs to be popular."[24] Even educators who are comfortable with the expectation that content-specific instruction must be mixed with social-emotional learning may not be willing to go the next step and open the door to the content of what troubles young people beneath the surface.

BOUNDEDNESS

Children in distress—and all children—need to feel cared for within the boundaries of a community that hears and sees them for who they are and what they're feeling. Most high school teachers will acknowledge that one of their roles is to notice, to listen—and to indicate to school administration, the guidance counselor, or parents if there is some concern. Schools can support this kind of listening in myriad ways. Advisory programs can play an important role, providing structure for a teacher and a small group of students to know and to listen to each other in a nonacademic setting. Disciplinary interventions grounded in restorative practice can also be an effective means of listening to the whole child.

In this vein, many educators advocate for restorative justice in schools. The contemporary efforts of urban educators—in New York City, Oakland, and other cities—have been especially effective in driving restorative justice reforms nationwide. It is important work, for these are disciplinary interventions that cultivate authentic conversations about motivation and sincere reflection on how a person's actions impact others. These forums can give young people reasons and tools for choosing differently next time, ways of understanding and redirecting their aggressive impulses. Such efforts help young people feel heard and understood within the bounds of a community that knows them well.

There are some very traditional school structures that can also play a role in honoring the whole child and channeling the aggressive drive. Traditional school athletics can do this. Physical exertion and release is part of the picture, but more important factors are the team and how the team is coached. Coached the wrong way, a culture of brutality can blossom in the subculture of school athletics: hazing, locker-room bullying, and dehumanizing opponents. But done right, athletics can be a civilizing force, channeling aggression through physical exertion and combat-like encounters bounded by the parameters of sportsmanship.

Boundaries and boundedness are key concepts here. The rituals, routines, loyalties, and uniforms of the team can help young people feel connected, contained, and stable, achieving a degree of identity clarity in a time of identity confusion. Erik Erikson discusses the adolescent need for identity parameters or boundaries that help youth "keep themselves together." He is discussing another social feature typical of school life: cliques—which, like teams, have significant potential for cruelty:

> To keep themselves together, adolescents temporarily overidentify, to the point of apparent complete loss of identity, with the heroes of cliques and crowds. . . . They become remarkably clannish, intolerant, and cruel in their exclusion of others who are "different," in skin color or cultural background, in tastes and gifts, and often in entirely petty aspects of dress and gesture. [25]

Erikson goes on to explain that this cruelty has its roots in the need to fend off—and build boundaries against—identity confusion, so intrinsic to adolescence:

> It is important to understand (which does not mean to condone or participate in) such intolerance as the necessary defense against a sense of identity confusion, which is unavoidable at a time of life when the body changes its propor-

tions radically, when genital maturity floods body and imagination with all manner of drives . . . and when life lies before one with a variety of conflicting possibilities and choices.[26]

Teams and clubs are ways that schools can help adolescents defend against identity confusion and meet their need for group belonging. Cliques and teams can be cruel and intolerant, but with good guidance they can be positive social forces: teenagers working toward a common goal, bounded and secured in the context of shared values, similarity of dress, and commonality of sign and symbol.

CURRICULUM REFORM

Meeting the needs of the whole child, however, cannot be an extracurricular effort alone. Advisory programs, restorative justice, counseling, coaching, teams, after-school clubs: these topics have been treated here only briefly, but they are very important. Each of these structures offers a context for honoring the whole child, addressing important identity needs, and channeling the aggressive drive productively. They are, however, extracurricular. They don't yet bring us into that arena of school life where most kids and teachers spend the majority of their time—the classroom.

In contemporary school reform literature, "differentiated instruction" is a term that perhaps best encapsulates those approaches to pedagogy that ensure that all students are engaged at appropriate levels of readiness and challenge. Thoughtful accommodations for learning disabilities are another essential component of pedagogy that honors the individual learner's needs.

Good teaching techniques like these are essential to a classroom community where every child feels valued, but the second part of this book will focus less on *how* we teach and more on *what* we teach. In school reform circles, adequate attention is being paid to pedagogical reforms that ensure the school knows and tends to each child's identity as an academic learner. There is less attention paid to curriculum content that tends to each child's identity as a person.

In many schools across the country, a young woman with pain in her heart can walk through the doors, go to advisory with a teacher who knows her well, check in about her weekend, smile at those who smile at her, briefly meet with a counselor to discuss her program of study, and go to four, five, six, or seven classrooms in her day, encountering engaging academic exercises and various teachers who deeply care about her—and yet not once hear an invitation to talk, write, or think about what she is really feeling inside.

And too, many of these girls then go home to quietly and diligently do their homework and just as quietly and diligently cut at their arms or thighs to feel some outer confirmation of the reality of the pain inside.

Or there's a boy who walks those same halls and then leaves school looking for some tool—fist, stick, knife, rock, gun—with which to work out his aggression. He's got "anger management issues," he might say, and he's trying to use that anger to break something other than his own already busted sense of self-worth. Or maybe he dulls the pain with drugs, and punishes the body/self simultaneously. Twemlow notes that young people use these "bodily experiences, alcohol, drugs, physical violence, and crime, to provide themselves with the sense of consolidation and coherent identity."[27] Yes, a coherent identity is what the child is seeking—and curriculum content has a role to play.

FOUR CURRICULUM REFORM IMPERATIVES

If aggression is a drive, and identity confusion is common, and criminality is a developmental phase, then a typical day in secondary school needs to offer students more than disembodied, abstract academic activities and a handful of cordial relationships. We need to open up the very content of the classroom to the emotional life of the whole child. Such a curriculum, calibrated to the identity journey of adolescence, will adhere to one or more of the following imperatives:

1. Invite and model the exploration of inner life
2. Foment ideological dissonance and commitment
3. Nourish self-awareness and self-control
4. Cultivate dexterity in using adult tools to approach adult tasks

In other words, this is curriculum that is willing to get personal, get political, get meta, and get to work. Young people need a curriculum like this—in addition to a healthy after-school culture, humane disciplinary interventions, solid guidance and advisory structures, and pedagogy that values each learner's skills. An ambitious curriculum of this kind is key to channeling adolescent aggression and destructiveness in directions that are good for young people and their communities.

We live in an age of upheaval, a time of declining life expectancies, systemic racism, mass incarceration, increased socioeconomic segregation, and environmental crisis. Social despair and dislocation perpetrates great pain and uncertainty upon children. Those troubles, which can be especially acute during the age of upheaval that is adolescence, generate energies that need to go somewhere.

Curriculum content that adheres to the four imperatives we will explore in the following chapters is an essential yet underutilized means of helping young people choose productive, life-affirming paths for what can otherwise become harmful ideas and energies.

QUESTIONS FOR REFLECTION AND DISCUSSION

1. Do you know any young people who, as Erikson says, engage in bad or hurtful behaviors in order to avoid feeling like "not-quite-some-body?" What do you think makes them feel like "not-quite-some-body" in the first place?
2. Have you ever been a part of a community that experienced a homicide in school or a homicidal threat? How did the school respond, and what was learned from it? Or, what lessons have you drawn from the school shootings reported in the press from other places?
3. How do the roles of bully, victim, and bystander play out in your schools and communities? How do these roles play out among children? Among youth? Among adults?
4. This chapter argues that if aggression is a drive, and identity confusion is common, and criminality is a developmental phase, then we need to open up the very content of the classroom to the emotional life of the whole child. Do you agree? Why or why not?

Part II

Only the Tiresome Classes?

Paradoxically, anger soon gave way to a profound feeling of liberation. Being able to write about lynching liberated me from being confined by it.
—James H. Cone, *The Cross and the Lynching Tree* (Maryknoll, NY: Orbis Books: 2013), xviii.

Chapter Five

GET PERSONAL

Schools can change the experience of rage through a consistent social attentiveness to the meanings of each child.

—Ann Marie Sacramone[1]

Urban youth who enter schools seeing themselves as smart and capable are confronted by curriculum that is blind to their realities.

—Christopher Emdin[2]

The first of our imperatives is to get personal. Classrooms must invite and model the exploration of inner life. When we express what's inside, holding our questions and pains up to the right public mirrors, our worth and power expand as we see our humanity reflected in the eyes of others.

How can a young person develop a coherent identity if key pieces to that identity puzzle, including difficult doubts and questions, are closeted or buried in shame?

The students that cut, swagger, stumble, and seethe each have stories to tell, and if we can help them tell their stories effectively, we reduce the risk that their strivings for a sense of self will end in the easy certainty of harm to self or others.

The school day had ended and the principal, Mr. Dalton, called Ms. Stevens, the middle school counselor, to ask if she could join him and the World Languages department to discuss next year's middle school offerings. With a heavy voice she said no, that she was still recovering from what had just happened in her office.

Mr. Dalton was curious and concerned, but Ms. Stevens was in the middle of processing the event with another school counselor, so Mr. Dalton resolved to contact her later to learn more. The next morning he went to her office and she wasn't there. She was next door, behind a closed door, again with her colleague, still reflecting on all that had happened yesterday, which included news of a recent graduate's suicide attempt as well as whatever had happened at the end of the day in her office. It had been a difficult week.

Later that day, Ms. Stevens told Mr. Dalton what had so troubled her the day before: a middle school girl convulsing on the floor of her office. It wasn't a seizure, and the girl wasn't choking. She was tearing out her hair, convulsively crying, writhing on the floor. It was the inside coming out, an emotional unraveling.

A call had been made, and a reluctant family member had been dispatched by the mother to get her child. The mother had been on the phone moments before, telling the daughter how "we don't want to go down this road again." Perhaps this was a reference to years earlier, Ms. Stevens thought, when the girl had been hospitalized in elementary school. This girl had been struggling for years with the trauma that had haunted her from her early childhood. On speakerphone, the mother told Ms. Stevens and the girl that someone would come get her, take her home, and that they could "have some ice cream and watch a movie."

Ms. Stevens affirmed that the girl's pain was hard to witness, but it was the mother's comments that were most unsettling. The mother was greeting the child's distress with a kind of "still face," a lack of acknowledgment of the urgency of the child's meaning. On top of witnessing the emotional turmoil of the child, Ms. Stevens went home that day wondering if the family was going to do anything at all to acknowledge the pain the child was feeling, and get her help.

"CIVIC STILL FACE"

What happens to a child when the caregivers do not recognize the inner meanings and feelings of the child? A parallel question can be asked of institutions and organizations that work with children. What happens when our childcare institutions—including schools—neglect to recognize and honor the inner life of the child? In both cases, it's pretty simple. This kind of neglect is a kind of harm, and often kids will internalize it and direct their own forms of violence on themselves or others. Mary Brady, whose discussion of cutting is referenced in chapter 1, notes that "the adolescent's pull to a self-destructive action is often related to a familial inability to grapple with major emotional situations."[3]

Analyst Ann Marie Sacramone spoke at the American Psychoanalytic Association's annual meeting in 2017. She has spent much time in schools, and describes our nation's civic institutions as "interactive partners that on social or biological levels either recognize and respond, or do not recognize and respond" to the people they serve. If there is recognition and response, the result is peace in the community; if there is no recognition and response, the result is violence. Sacramone notes that when our institutions "turn a civic still face to expressions of distress," the resulting violence can be directed in outward or inward directions. She goes on to ask, "When environmental recognition and response is absent, do our communities scratch away at themselves?"[4]

"Scratch away at themselves" is a reference to the work of Dr. Beatrice Beebe, whose study of mother-infant recognition and attachment patterns involves rigorous documentation of mother-child interactions on film: frame-by-frame, second-by-second paired images of their interactions. In these films, Sacramone notes, "one sees the developing calm or joyful excitement that infants feel when interactions with their caregiver reflect play with the meanings of each partner."

The mother's communications and baby's gestures and vocalizations each reflect something of the other. This is not an exact mirroring and it does not happen all of the time, but it happens enough that each partner feels secure. "Conversely," says Sacramone, "when the caregiver's response reflects their own past trauma, instead of a recognition of the infant's meaning, one may see early aggression and violence in the infant's digging into her own skin with her nails."[5]

Later, after the episode of the convulsing child tearing out her own hair, Ms. Stevens came to see Mr. Dalton. She told him the relatively good news that the family had decided to take their daughter, again, to a residential placement for psychiatric care. How temporary or long term, Ms. Stevens didn't know, but hopefully the child's crisis would lead to better care and mental health in the long run.

This one girl's crisis is yet another extreme case of an adolescent in distress, but as has been noted, a crisis can teach us a lot about the ordinary. At a very basic level, every child needs to see reciprocity of feeling and recognition of meaning reflected in the face of caregivers. This is a basic need that endures throughout the life cycle, and meeting that need is an obligation of all caregivers, including educators.

LIBERAL ARTS INCLUDE THE CHILD

Teens Who Hurt, by Ken Hardy and Tracey Laszloffy, is a book full of insight and careful listening to young people who do violence to themselves and others. The framework of the authors is simple, but not simplistic:

Devaluation + Disruption of Community + Dehumanization of Loss = Rage

And "rage," Hardy and Laszloffy write, "is a natural and inevitable response to experiences of pain and injustice. When rage is channeled constructively, it can be a positive and transformative force. However, when rage is denied expression or treated as if it is negative, it intensifies and usually culminates in an eruption of violence."[6]

High school in America offers a liberal arts education. College, career, and citizenship preparation anchor our mission statements, and our even broader charge is to help students understand the diverse dimensions of what it means to be a human being on this earth. Science, history, and art—these required subjects—each comprise the widest of domains.

It's silly to believe we can cover it all, but it's important to believe that with the daunting whole of human experience as our subject, part of our work is to reckon with painful realities, past and present, collective and personal. Into the curriculum must enter the lives and feelings of people who have been devalued, injustices that have not yet been righted, losses not yet mourned. It is in everyone's best interest that we do this, for to neglect the reality of rage—individual or collective—and to be silent about injustice—personal or societal—is dangerous. Hardy and Laszloffy offer warning:

> If the response to rage involves a sustained and systemic effort to suppress or deny it, this greatly increases the probability that rage will lead to an explosion of violence. The process of suppressing and/or denying rage may create the appearance on the surface that all is calm and secure. But this calm is merely the calm before the storm.[7]

A school's core academic classes can provide opportunities for rage to find constructive channels, and to construct curriculum content with this in mind is entirely within the parameters of a school's charge. To connect academic skill building to personal topics safely and effectively—in any classroom and in any content area—teachers can keep in mind four simple priorities:

1. Establishment of trust
2. Modeling and exposure
3. Invitation, not coercion
4. Validation and praise

GET PERSONAL: FOUR PRIORITIES

1. Establishment of Trust

In the earliest phases of human development, establishing trust in the goodness of the world and trust in one's own goodness is the best foundation for everything else to come. The child must trust that crucial needs will be met by the adults and the environment. Through the way that the adults respond to the child, the child should come to believe that adults are trustworthy and that the child herself is worthy of protection and nourishment. Classroom communities—the teacher, the individual child, and the group—need to follow the same developmental trajectory as they cohere as a new entity in a new relationship.

The positional authority of the adult in the room—the teacher—is an essential ingredient of a Get Personal pedagogy. The careful use of authority should not be confused with authoritarianism. It should be clearly established up front that the positional power in the room will be used to equitably enable the powerful voices of others.

All of this happens in the first weeks or months of the class. Group work should wait. The classroom community benefits when the teacher maintains a whole-class format of interaction for the majority of the trust-building period. This can take some time and should not be rushed. The whole-class format should be in a circle or square or "U," some shape that allows the adult to see the faces of every student in the room, and allows students to see and interact with each other as much as with the adult.

In the early weeks and months of a course, the adult must demonstrate that breaches of norms will not be tolerated, that voices that take risks will be heard and never be ridiculed. There is no prescription for tone or tactic here, only that it must be done. Students should not be divided into self-governing groups until the norms of whole-group governance have been established with the teacher. An authority cannot be delegated and distributed unless it exists.

Teachers who have a proclivity toward student-centered classrooms may question this emphasis on the positional authority of the teacher, but it can't be questioned that we learn from modeling and the guidance of elders as much as through experimentation and self-guided discovery. This is not to say that inquiry-based instruction isn't essential here. Norms, for instance, can be developed in constructivist collaboration with the class. A teacher should know in which direction, however, this process needs to lead. Some useful norms for the Get Personal classroom can be:

- *One mic* (or, *Don't talk when others are talking*): This may be the Golden Rule. It should be followed in any classroom that wants to evoke personal expression. To ensure that every voice is heard, value every voice.
- *Avoid absolutes:* It is all too easy to alienate someone or some group of people when we casually use absolutes like "all," "always," "every," and similar wording. Generalizations that use words like "most" or "often" are safer.

- *"I" statements*: Speak from your own personal truth and personal experience. Also, acknowledge the personal statements of others.

Other norms can be developed with the class, and norms such as these can be amended to reflect terminology with which the students are familiar. In one of the classes referenced above, a film class in which Karen made a film about youth depression, the teachers used the first weeks and months to establish norms like these, and occasionally the instructors needed to use their positional power to reinforce them. They took their time. It was a full semester—half the year—before the teachers asked students to commit to a topic for their own individual film projects. The students did a lot of writing, talking, and sharing in those first months, but there was teacher direction and much emphasis on modeling and exposure. It is important to offer examples of young people and adults maturely discussing personal and sometimes painful topics, and to develop with the students a shared vocabulary for talking to each other about such topics.

2. Modeling and Exposure

Youth Communication, a youth-centric publishing house in New York City referenced in the first chapter, offers compilations of writing by teenagers on countless topics of contemporary relevance to young people. The geographic context for the writing is typically urban, but the themes transcend place specificity and include essays and stories about a multitude of young adult challenges.

The instructors of Karen's film class read several essays from Youth Communication with their students. These personal essays were one of several ways the adults demonstrated to the students that people can talk about and externalize their pains and questions.

Killing pain, fleeing from it, or blaming and assailing others for it are the dominant ways young people see adults handling pain today. They need other models of how to bear hurt and sorrow. In the era of opioids and other medications that can sometimes dull the senses too much, children need to be explicitly taught that a painkiller is only one way to handle pain. Pain can also be given voice.

In addition to youth voices, like those of the Youth Communication authors, students benefit from exposure to adult models of how to explore personal topics: films, literature, testimonials, and psychological texts like *Teens Who Hurt*. Just as kids need to see and hear other kids giving voice to stories like those they carry inside themselves, the students likewise need exposure to unsensationalized, unsanitized, yet intellectualized and elegant representations of a person's interior life.

It is informative to look back at the content teachers brought to the table in Karen's film class, and what stories the young people eventually chose to tell—about themselves and about others. There are strong correlations.

Early in the year, the instructors brought in a film about stress made by students in another school. One boy in the class later wrote a story about the stress he feels in his family in the years since the death of his mother.

David, the English teacher, designed a unit in which students read a trio of short stories by Ernest Hemingway: *Hills Like White Elephants, A Simple Enquiry*, and *The Sea Change*. Each of these very short stories is heavy in dialogue, rich in opportunities for interpretation, offering fine portrayals of complex conversations about important topics: homosexuality, pregnancy, abortion, gender, and power. These stories were carefully read and discussed. One of the students in the class later made a film about being gay and coming out. Another student made a film about teen pregnancy.

The class also spent time with the Adverse Childhood Effects study, research that powerfully demonstrates correlations between childhood troubles and risks to well-being later in life. A doctor came to the class to discuss the biological side of addiction and recovery. One student in the class later made a film about addiction in the community and its impact on families. And Karen made her film about teen depression, a topic the instructors had honored with a roundtable discussion earlier in the year at which a local therapist and former client talked about self-harm, depression, and the client's path to wellness.

When adults offer models of how to respectfully share and listen to personal stories, young people will learn from the example.

3. Invitation, Not Coercion

It is good to clearly state the expectation that students will approach topics that can be personal and difficult to discuss. It is important to offer modeling and exposure, but no one should be told they have to tell their own story. There is no need to create a climate of pressure for students to get personal when there has been modeling and intentional work to build a safe classroom climate, with norms and vocabulary for talking about sensitive topics. In such an environment, an invitation to tell your story is all that's needed for some to seize the occasion. This kind of teaching can help give students names for what they are feeling inside and a possible opportunity to have it externalized, objectified.

If we can name it, we own it more, and it owns us less. And when we share with others, and sense their empathy, we feel less alone and therefore less shame. Karen's film about depression was indeed shared, along with all the other films from the class—shared with each other and with a large community audience at a local theater at the end of the year. And they continued to be shown in the following months and years at school and various forums in the community. The film about addiction, for instance, was shown at a local town hall, paired with another professionally made film on the same topic. The film about coming out was shown at a local LGBTQ Pride festival, again paired with the showing of a film created by professionals.

The public viewings of student work are affirming, a public reflection of worth and recognition, like the interaction between the infant and the caregiver, whose face responds to the infant in recognition rather than turning away or being still. When students do personal work and then commune with an audience who responds and affirms, the young people can see how their pain—to paraphrase James Baldwin—may be precisely what connects them to the rest of humankind.

4. Validation and Praise

Before any public audience for student work, first there is the audience of the teacher and the classroom. Once the children are engaged in telling their own stories, or—in science, social studies, and other subjects—producing products to which they have personal connections, the adult in the room must model the giving of specific feedback and public praise. The adult should also coach and guide the other young people in the room to do the same.

Err on the side of abundant praise, at first. When trust has been established and the class or particular individuals are ready for it, then critical feedback can be offered as well. Again, educators must take our time. Tell students that the focus is going to be on the positive first, because as they enter into revisions, it's important to know what works so that they don't discard good work.

When it comes to creating a classroom audience for the written word, a particularly powerful practice is to have confident and fluent readers showcase the work of students. Whether it's an essay, a research paper, a poem, or a story, many young people may be able to come up with a beautiful turn of phrase or well-crafted paragraph on paper, but they may not have any of the reading, speaking, or presentation skills to share that work in an effective way with a public audience.

Invite other adults—or even older, more mature students—who have practice and dexterity with the spoken word to read the work of students. It can bring life and dignity to work that otherwise might be spoken in rushed or hushed or clumsy articulations. It also allows the authors to hear their ideas from a new perspective. Above all, reading the work of students allows their voices to be heard in a public forum at a time when their own self-consciousness about voice, physical appearance, and social status might make reading their own work too fraught a risk to take. This is an especially powerful way to validate the work of less sophisticated writers. A practiced reader can know where to put a pause, even if the child doesn't know where to put a comma.

For students who are too insecure or private to want their work to be shared by others, it is always worth offering them the chance to have their work shared anonymously. Deep inside all of us, the stories that reside there want to be told to someone, somehow, at some time. Of course, educators must guard personal information of students very carefully; indeed, sometimes an adult may need to question whether the words a child is willing or wanting to share ought to be made public. We must always ask ourselves, and the student: Is it really appropriate or safe to share this?

At the same time, we mustn't let confidentiality be a constraint that limits students to no audience other than the teacher. There is a confessional impulse that is strong in most people. And it is strong for good reason: the healing force of having a personal story heard and affirmed in the right context or community is unquestionable.

EVEN THOSE WHO STAY SILENT

If there are teens who hurt in our classrooms—and there are—a curriculum that carefully gets personal is one way that some of those students can have their loss humanized, their experiences valued, and community created. Thus there are fewer reasons for these students to do violence to themselves or others.

A Get Personal classroom is worth the effort even if some young people say nothing—they will still sense from the modeling and validation of others' stories that the kind of life they've lived is not a cause for shame. Teachers should affirm that confession is powerful, but that it is also acceptable to keep your past and your personal life private. A few students will never feel that the classroom community is the right place to tell their story— but when adults communicate that what's inside every person is important, it is more likely a child will take advantage of other forums to speak, such as a private conversation with the teacher, a friend, a counselor, or a family member.

Shame, rage, nihilism, sadness—and the root causes of such feelings—all have a place as topics explored in school. It takes fortitude, and there is no formula, but the pedagogy for reaching and teaching the whole child is not complicated. Establishing trust is the first step; then comes modeling and exposure, then invitation—not coercion—and then validation and praise. Any teacher with willingness and patience can adapt curriculum and adopt pedagogy that acknowledge the holes and hungers of adolescence, turning private pain into public assertions of power.

OUT OF THE CLOSET, INTO THE COMMONS

Tammy was a girl who in her ninth-grade year seemingly intentionally got caught with illegal substances in school. The previous weeks and months had been tumultuous at home. Police were getting used to calls from Tammy's aunt, her guardian. The department for children's services was involved. The school counselor and administration were becoming unsure of what to say when Tammy's family would call with their "we-don't-know-what-to-do-she's-out-of-control" lamentations.

Tammy was indeed behaving in ways that suggested her family had little capacity for controlling her ways. She was violent at home, came and went as she pleased, had been in state custody once already in the past year, and was being very closely monitored by child welfare authorities. The younger children in the home were one of their main concerns.

Tammy knew she was on thin ice. She knew that if she was suspended from school again she might be removed from her home, or what semblance of home there was for her then. And she took the steps she needed to take to make it happen.

On this day, she'd left class and knew her principal was looking for her with the suspicion she was carrying drugs. She was close to the back doors of the school, and could have easily walked out and ditched whatever she was carrying. Instead she came back down the hallway toward the principal, cursed him and the school, and stood there posturing loudly with great defiance and profanity. But when she was told to come to the office, she complied. Then she was searched, the stuff was found, the family and police were notified.

She was then removed from her home. It wasn't simply because of this particular incident; there were other more extreme and very high-risk behaviors that led to her no longer being in her home and at the school—or at any regular public school. The family and school were in fact thankful for the state's intervention, thankful that all of this happened when she was young enough for state agencies to mobilize. If she had been in tenth or eleventh grade, the agencies might have seen her as too old to be a priority.

When she was younger, her middle school teachers found it hard to get to know Tammy as a student. She never did any work. She refused to produce work even in small group or one-on-one settings with educators whom she'd come to trust. But at the end of the year, her science, social studies, and English teachers collaborated to design a unit of study that focused on community wellness. The unit culminated in a form of Socratic seminar, a student-to-student dialogue that probes the essential questions of the unit.

The seminar was a culminating assessment, and the students prepared for it for weeks. It included a "ticket to participate," which was a long "graphic organizer" or form on which students document their preparations, their ideas, and the evidence to substantiate their claims. The English teacher helped prepare students for the discussion—how to ask clarifying and probing questions, how to show active listening, how to follow other norms—and the social studies and science teachers helped the students explore the content of the unit. One topic the science teacher explored with students is the brain science of addiction, and it was in responding to a prompt about addiction that Tammy, for the first time all year, wrote something.

It was in a one-on-one setting with her special education teacher that she began to write. Tammy had an Individualized Education Plan, and reading and writing were areas in which she struggled. She was a proud person, not willing to show public signs of weakness. She never read aloud or participated in class discussions. But when this topic was explored in her classes, a topic with great personal meaning, she finally decided to write.

Her mother, whom she ever longed to see but couldn't, struggled with addiction, and this invitation to explore this topic brought Tammy's story out of the closet of shame and into the light of public space.

- Her special education teacher played a big role here, especially in the establishment of trust, born of consistency of care and expectations.
- Her English teacher helped through the journal prompts, the poems they read, the possibility of anonymous expression, and the expectation for public talk. Her social studies teacher helped by putting personal struggles with addiction into broader public policy contexts, normalizing the discussion of a topic that often generates painful feelings.
- Her science teacher helped by naming heroin and opioids as examples of substances or experiences to which the body can become addicted in its normal effort to know pleasure and comfort, again normalizing and humanizing a topic that often comes with feelings of derision and other-ness.

This girl's potentially shame-laden story suddenly became a story willing to be told, because the story could see that its loneliness was an illusion and that, in fact, other people live the story, too.

THE PERSONAL IS POLITICAL

We can get personal in superficial ways, or we can get personal in ways that correspond to deeper needs: the basic needs of families, the identity needs of individuals, the socioeconomic, cultural, and environmental needs of the broader society. Tammy's teachers connected the curriculum to a deeper layer of relevance when they brought the needs and troubles of the community into the classroom. The topic had urgency for both the individual and for her community: the wellness of one was connected to the wellness of others. It was thus a political as well as a personal exploration.

When we get personal in ways that correspond to more profound needs, we will often find that we are simultaneously stepping into the realm of the political. My story, your story, his or her story then becomes *our* story and history, relevant to us all.

A contemporary painter, Titus Kaphar, affirms this notion in an anecdote he tells about his evolution as an artist. Among the work for which Kaphar is best known is a painting of a painting. It presents a portrait of Thomas Jefferson on a canvas that has come undone, folding and falling away. Behind the image of Jefferson emerges another portrait, an image of Sally Hemings, unclothed. Hemings is a woman who was enslaved at Jefferson's home and with whom he had a sexual relationship. Kaphar is an artist unafraid to tear at the fabric of history and reveal truths that many prefer stay buried.

In a public radio program, *On Being with Krista Tippett*, Kaphar once discussed the period in his studies when he began to see that standard art history courses were inadequately representing the work of African American and other non-white people who have shaped the history of artistic expression in our country. Kaphar says, "It became very clear to me that if I wanted to know that history, I was going to have to seek it out on my own." The program host then asks if this is when he took the paintbrush into his own hands and began creating his own work. Kaphar suggests that he'd already been painting, but that this moment was indeed a crossroads, saying, "I think people would say that's when the work got political." Then he adds: "I say that's when the work got personal."[8]

QUESTIONS FOR REFLECTION AND DISCUSSION

1. In your experience, what happens to a child when the caregivers do not adequately recognize and respond to the child's needs and feelings? What happens when our childcare institutions—including schools—neglect to honor the inner life of the child?

2. Are adults in your school or community willing and able to offer young people models of how to share and listen to personal stories? In what contexts does this happen effectively? Are more efforts needed in this area? What are the risks of adults sharing too much personal information with children?

3. Do you agree that shame, rage, nihilism, sadness—and the root causes of such feelings—all have a place as topics in school? Why or why not?

4. Do any of the four guidelines for the Get Personal classroom seem appropriate to implement in your school context? Why or why not? What benefits might there be? What concerns?

Chapter Six

GET POLITICAL

If the central goal of schools were to prepare students to engage productively in a democracy, then students would be working on the concerns of their immediate and future life and on the concerns of their immediate and extended communities.

—Carl Glickman[1]

When schools model and invite the exploration of inner life, what students carry on the inside can be outwardly affirmed. Losses can be acknowledged and mourned. Questions carried alone can become collective inquiry. And this process of collectivizing questions and concerns has inherently political dimensions, because any shared concern exists within a social and political context.

The political is a domain that includes every aspect of our lives, from clean water and trash collection to healthcare and war-making. A healthy democracy needs its citizens to wrestle with and criticize the decisions of elected officials and the actions of powerful people and groups that shape our lives. Schools have a crucial role in the education of informed citizens, and this role is particularly aligned with the developmental capacity of adolescents: curriculum that gets political is a means for adolescents to find identity coherence in times of great uncertainty.

The potentially extreme dispositions of youth, their capacity for destruction, their rude willing and desiring, can be turned productively toward targets that need assailing and contesting, such as unjust public policies and corrupt institutions. It comes with risk, but channeling the force of youth in productive political directions is in everyone's interest. Consider that young people in our country today have better access to weapons that kill than most other children anywhere else in the world. This makes typical adolescent aggression atypically dangerous, for if they have an impulse to destroy some-thing or someone, they can easily find the lethal weapons to do it.

Instead, we need our children to choose ideology to use to break things, to attack unfairness in nonviolent political arenas, rather than attack their communities or their own bodies. This is why we must create curriculum that gets political. We must create forums in the classroom for ideological disso-nance and debate, as well as opportunities that lead to empowerment through application and action outside the classroom.

The young adult violence and criminal behaviors that we seek to prevent are cousin to other rough impulses animating adolescence, ones that we ought to permit. This includes the revolutionary disruption of established social norms, policies, structures. This rebelliousness is something that any healthy democratic society must endure. Youth have a special role to play in a soci-ety's evolution.

Adolescent nihilists are few. The norm is the adolescent inclined toward strong beliefs, allegiances, and loyalties—fidelity to teams, heroes, ideolo-gies, and ideas. Curriculum can be instrumental in cultivating ideological commitment. Curriculum can help guide young people to acts of socially healthy resistance and rebellion.

FIDELITY TO IDEALS

In adolescence, as Erik Erikson notes, "the tables of childhood dependence begin slowly to turn: no longer is it merely for the old to teach the young the meaning of life. It is the young who, by their responses and actions, tell the old whether life as represented to them has some vital promise, and it is the young who carry in them the power to confirm those who confirm them, to renew and regenerate, to disavow what is rotten, to reform and rebel."[2] In adolescence, a "seeking after an inner coherence and a durable set of values can always be detected."[3]

Fidelity is Erikson's term for the character trait that emerges from this seeking: "Fidelity is the ability to sustain loyalties freely pledged in spite of the inevitable contradictions of value systems. It is the cornerstone of identity and receives inspiration from confirming ideologies and affirming compan-ions."[4] Ideological commitment is thus an important part of adolescent self-hood.

Educators should facilitate the taking of stands, carefully providing young people with ideological options, cultivating ideological dissonance and de-bate, inviting them to take sides in informed, rigorous, evidence-based ways. We should help them understand that this is what democracy needs, and that their role—with the fresh eyes of youth—is to declare what is outdated and name what needs changing.

BRAVE OUTLET

If schools are not placing the content of our classes into contexts where there can be mature debates about moral, social, and political topics, we are not providing adolescents a productive context for tearing down and building up, for channeling their destructive impulses. It is not a question of whether that destructiveness gets channeled, but by what channel. The poet Robert Frost makes a simple observation: "blood will out." And from that same poem, "The Flood":

> [P]ower of blood itself releases blood.
> It goes by might of being such a flood
> Held high at so unnatural a level.
> It will have outlet, brave and not so brave. [5]

Our curriculum can provide opportunities for the blood to boil bravely. We want these bodies in our classrooms: eyes open, hands in the air, legs bouncing, cheeks flushed, voices resonant with the emotion of strong belief—maybe not every day, but on many days. Nearly every topic in the world and in every schoolhouse can be placed in the context of a moral or ethical question that raises blood pressure and gives adolescent energy brave outlet.

BEFORE THE AFTERMATH

In February 2018, much of the nation watched Emma González, a senior at Marjory Stoneman Douglas High School (MSDHS) in Parkland, Florida, introduce herself to the world by waving in her hands notes from her Advanced Placement U.S. Government class, on which she'd written points for her impassioned remarks. She spoke about this AP class, and how the students would study to make sure that their "arguments based on politics and political history are watertight." She told the world, "The students at this school have been having debates on guns for what feels like our entire lives." [6]

She was speaking in the aftermath of the murder of fourteen children and three staff members at her school. She and her classmates spoke with passionate purpose about the topic of gun control. Our nation heard their voices amplified across the land.

Like Black Lives Matter and other recent uprisings, these youth protests are a movement born of bloodshed and passionate outrage. But there was another catalyst for the youth-led gun control movement that stands out—not for its brutality or the media attention, but for its banality: the quiet, quotidian labor of the teacher planning lessons.

MSDHS student Jaclyn Corin was also ready to defend her convictions with knowledge when the terrible time came, in part due to the classes she'd taken. The New Yorker reported that she was "prepared to advocate for gun-law reform, having worked on a fifty-page project about gun control for her AP composition-and-rhetoric class a couple of months before."[7]

Jeff Foster was the AP Government teacher at the school. Journalist Jorge Rivas reports that on the very day his students' peers were killed, Foster had conducted a lesson on special interest groups, including the National Rifle Association (NRA):

> His lesson plan that day included a discussion about the Columbine and Sandy Hook school shootings, with emphasis on how every politician comes out [after] a tragedy to say the right thing about changing gun regulation. The students learned how the NRA goes to work as soon [as] news reporters and the public move on to the next story.[8]

This is a teacher who is committed to the whole child and to the whole society in which that child is growing up. His vision and hope, writes Rivas, is that students will leave his class "and vote, run for office, or join a special interest group for an issue they care about."[9] He has prepared them for this and more. It is important to contemplate work that this teacher engages in as he plans his curriculum, and the work that this teacher asks of his students: the extensive research and writing; the debates; the complex, serious, critical thinking.

In mid-March of 2018, students around the nation walked out of their schools in acts of student-organized solidarity with victims of school violence. Many teachers walked with them. But this kind of solidarity is not enough. If educators wish to engage with students in political action on school time, that work is about more than following students outside for a few minutes. It's about hours designing lesson plans and carefully framing our projects to ensure that students of all identity backgrounds find a point of entry into the work. It's about days of lessons dedicated to rigorous and engaging debates, and sometimes-hefty research papers that help students understand contemporary challenges and historical context. It's about deliberately and carefully helping students build knowledge of how public policy, and legislation shape their world. It's about showing students how, in every part of our lives—from how we labor and where we live, to how we learn and whom we love—we are shaped by circumstances that are shaped by policy choices, past and present.

When we help our students see how power works, we help them see how they can use the tools of their own power to make their world a better place. "Legislation may not change the hearts of men," Dr. Martin Luther King Jr. told those who gathered at Grosse Pointe High School to hear him speak in 1968, but "it does change the habits of men."[10] New habits give new structure and meaning to our lives. They are how we change our world.

The student activism of 2018 brought about a movement electric with the idealism and energy of youth. After the day of walk-outs, many thousands of students traveled to Washington, DC, marching behind the banners of Emma González and hundreds of other young people, flags waving with outrage, remarks delivered with eloquence and policy demands. Educators who admire González and her peers must remember that the first flag she waved at the world, tears in her eyes and precision in her demands, was a stack of notes she wrote in history class.

"AX TO GRIND"

In the fall of 2017, several Vermont educators organized a gathering called "Personal Learning for the Common Good." The catalysts were several, including a conversation that one of the organizers, a school principal, had had with a teacher colleague.

She was a mid-career teacher who had recently moved to the region, hired by a school where she was encouraged to probe, through her teaching, the political dimensions of her content area. She told her principal that in all her years of experience, she'd never before been asked to place curriculum content in a political, ethical, or moral context. This should not be surprising. Most teachers' careers include few encouragements to place teaching and learning in a political context. The ivory tower is a safe place. The risks of leaving it are many. Teachers need an invitation to do this, and support.

The organizers of the conference promoted the occasion via e-mail and social media to their friends and professional networks. Here is some of the text of the promotional materials:

> Vermont's Personal Learning Plans ask students to reflect on their values and goals—but what about their rights and responsibilities as citizens?
>
> Our communities face problems of great substance, which our young citizens must start solving—now. Yet many educators feel unprepared or unsupported when it comes to designing action-oriented curriculum that delves into controversial contemporary challenges.
>
> Wage stagnation, youth flight, climate crisis, gun violence, opiate addiction, terrorism and war, child poverty, racial and class divisions. . . . What supports or incentives do school communities need in order to design curriculum that addresses pressing political, social, and environmental challenges?[11]

Not all responses to this initiative were favorable. Not everyone feels contemporary politics has a place in the schoolhouse. One of the organizers received this response to their outreach:

> See now this is a big part of what's wrong with public school education. Every political and social movement with an ax to grind sees the school system as a lever for its agenda—the hand that rocks the cradle acting on a captive audience of bidable, ignorant, inexperienced youth who can be coerced to your cause. There is precious little time in the school year to teach, you know, math, but schools are now supposed to "design curriculum [sic] that addresses pressing political, social and environmental challenges."
>
> And what happens when my kids are co-opted into a political movement I disagree with, funded by my tax dollars that are extracted from me at the point of a gun? You should not be surprised then when funding for the public school system loses public support. [12]

The writer of this e-mail was unlikely to attend the conference and engage in discussions of how schools can support students in contemporary problem solving. This is unfortunate, and there is a lesson to be learned from this exchange. If we want a diverse array of political perspectives at the table—if we want adults and children of all different backgrounds and beliefs to participate sincerely in the work—it matters how we frame the discussion. Instead of listing "gun violence," the organizers could have framed the issue more broadly, such as "gun rights and gun control." They might have gotten more diverse participants to the conference. Or what if, instead of the problem of "wage stagnation," they had framed this topic as "workforce development?" Wage stagnation could come up in the discussion, as well as income inequality more broadly, but the conversation would have had a broader band of the political spectrum sitting about the table.

Desegregating our conversations—and classrooms, schools, and neighborhoods—is among the most important paths to a healthy democracy. We want a diverse group of voices sounding in the debate, diverse by race, class, and belief. For this reason, it's important that educators don't appear to their communities as having an "ax to grind." It's just as important that we—educators and our school communities—don't shirk our duties to prepare students for the world that awaits and shapes them now.

CURRICULUM CONTENT THAT GETS POLITICAL

Indeed there is an unfair assumption behind the "ax to grind" comment, which suggests that public school educators are bringing politics into the classroom in ways other schools are not. Consider these excerpts from course descriptions pulled from the 2019–2020 course catalog of Exeter Academy, an elite private school:

- This course introduces students to the unique process by which American governments develop policies to address the nation's most significant problems. In addition to studying specific policy issues, students will read about Congress and the presidency, political parties, elections, ideologies, the role of media, and the psychology of politics.
- What is feminism and how is it expressed in literary texts? What does it mean to read literature through the lens of gender? This course will allow students to explore these and other questions central to feminist literary studies. Readings will include a range of literature by women as well as selected works of critical theory.
- This course explores the role of gender in shaping humans' identities and power structures in several twentieth-century circumstances around the world. Questions of political and legal rights, including emotional equity, public health, and definitions of marriage, as well as social issues, such as wearing a veil, family concerns, and work inside and outside the home may be considered.
- Does a corporation have responsibility beyond itself? Should the bottom line trump ethical considerations? Who or what protects the public interest? This course considers these questions in the world of business and management. Students debate moral aspects of institutional policies and practices, in regard to the environment, fair labor, executive compensation, globalization and international sweatshops, consumerism and its opponents, race and gender issues in the market, advertising, insider trading, whistle blowing, and the corporate responsibilities of multinational firms.
- This course will examine the plight of developing nations. Students will explore why the quality of life of these countries' citizens remains, in the aggregate, so low and their choices so limited. Topics to be considered include the historical legacy of colonization, cultural and social issues, geography and climate, agriculture and famine, human capital, governance and corruption, and foreign aid, debt, and trade.[13]

These are course descriptions written by teachers who are willing to take on contemporary political challenges through their curriculum. These are teachers who see their vocation as one that prepares students to be informed and powerful citizens in a democracy. There are challenges to this work—and ways to overcome them—which will be discussed, but first let's consider some other curriculum descriptions, this time from public schools.

Since its founding, the James Baldwin School (JBS) in New York City has partnered with several school-reform organizations that support the infusion of contemporary problem solving into the curriculum: the Coalition of Essential Schools, Expeditionary Learning, NYC Outward Bound, and the New York Performance Standards Consortium. Below are several course descriptions from the 2016–2017 school year:

- *Borders:* How open should our borders be? Today immigration policy is at the center of a boiling debate in this country. This academic expedition will explore the political, social, and economic significance of borders between countries. Students will combine their learning from historical immigration policies with their research on other immigration controversies in the United States, past or present . . .
- *Refugees:* A refugee is someone who fled his or her home and country because of "a well-founded fear of persecution because of his/her race, religion, nationality, membership in a particular social group, or political opinion," according to the United Nations 1951 Refugee Convention. Many refugees are in exile to escape the effects of natural or humanmade disasters. The term "refugee," like the people it describes, can cover a lot of ground. Politicians, aid workers, academics, and the press often approach the word from different angles, and with varying ideas of the rights, roles, and responsibilities the term implies. Such divergent views fuel the global debate about how best to manage and protect refugees, who by some counts number over 60 million and still counting . . .
- *Revolutionary Women:* This course is an exploration of women and girls as powerful individuals and changemakers throughout the world, past and present. Women often are left out of mainstream history or are confined to damaging stereotypes. Students will dig deeper for stories of radical and revolutionary women who have been making history all along. . . . The course will also engage students in seeking out and documenting the stories of women and girls in their own communities.
- *Math for Social Justice:* How can we use our knowledge of math to empower ourselves and our communities? How do advertisements and other media use numbers to influence our opinions? How can we use math as a tool to analyze our world? These questions and more will be looked at in this course. We will be using our knowledge of mathematics to go deeper into understanding social issues that we face every day. Some of the math topics we will learn about are statistics, graphing, compound interest, and budgeting.
- *Got Water:* Students will collect and analyze statistics based on the results from their water taste test. Students will find evidence to support the "Flint" water crisis. Students will use statistical techniques to analyze the lack of "drinkable" water as a global health concern in order to develop the abilities and confidence needed to analyze any subject. This expedition will culminate with a final action project regarding the "Flint" water crisis.
- *Native Son in the Promised Land:* Is racism still alive all over our country, from our big cities, to our small towns? If so, how does it operate systematically to place some in power and others (based on their race, gender, sexuality) on the outskirts with less power, value, and worth? How can it affect a person's psyche to be powerless and on the margins; to be consid-

ered a problem, an outcast, a menace? The class will explore what happens when one takes the quest to regain power back, into his or her own hands! What/Who is harmed?

- *Climate Change: Our New Normal:* Experts claim that climate change is upon us, is happening right now, but how do we experience climate on a day-to-day basis? And how will the "new normal" affect us in the future? We will look back into our climate past to get some perspective on the projected changes. We will also explore Earth systems interactions in urban areas to ensure our survival here in New York City, a vulnerable coastal region.[14]

The JBS offerings show how math and science educators can, like teachers in the humanities, place curriculum content in political and contemporary problem-solving context.

At a very different school in central Vermont, Randolph Union, there are similar courses, developed in the school's Project-Based Learning (PBL) Lab, which supports teachers in any discipline in designing curriculum that intentionally approaches contemporary challenges in collaboration with community partners and experts. Consider some of the PBL course descriptions for 2017–2018:

- *Climate Change: Is it too late for meaningful action?* Using global average temperature as a measurement, Earth's hottest year on record was 2014; that is, until the temperature record was shattered again in 2015. And now, according to a recent article published in the *New York Times*, 2016 temperatures "have blown past the previous record three years in a row." While El Niño helped fuel some of the rise in temperatures, this does not account for the overall trend: the fifteen hottest years have occurred within the last sixteen years (NASA). What does this information mean for us? The Climate Change PBL will investigate the root causes, mechanisms, and impacts of global warming and work with the community to investigate approaches and solutions.
- *Restorative Justice:* Do our schools and courts treat people fairly? Do VT schools discipline students fairly? Do some kinds of students get suspended more often than others? Does a school suspension have any connection to dropping out? And what about our legal system: Do the courts treat people fairly? Does VT have too many prisons—or not enough? Should people with mental health challenges go to jail if they commit a crime? How should people with opiate addiction be treated when in custody? In this PBL challenge, we will build on our previous successes and continue to raise and research questions like these.
- *Service Learning Abroad:* How do we work with a local nonprofit to make meaningful change in a country through service-learning work without

imposing our own beliefs? In this PBL challenge, students will learn, listen and act. The challenge is designed to research and familiarize students with the peoples, cultures and inherent beliefs of the countries where we choose to engage in service-learning work, while analyzing our own perceptions. Students will explore Nicaragua—the people, culture, cuisine, music, history and contemporary politics—in order to best understand and serve the needs of the families they will work with during a service-learning trip to that country. Students who enroll in this PBL will be part of the club that is going on the April 2018 Spanish Trip to Nicaragua. We will work with a community partner organization, Planting Hope, which has the goal to support "sustainable growth and mutual understanding through the exchange of social, cultural and material riches of Nicaragua and the U.S."[15]

There are obstacles to doing Get Political coursework well, not the least of which is finding the time and space. It is clear from some of the PBL Lab course descriptions—all of which can be taken to meet graduation standards in core content areas—that this school is integrating into the school day certain clubs and activities that typically float in after-school hours and extra-curricular spaces. In past years at the school, planning the international trip, developing a group of students trained in restorative justice practice, hosting the Interact club, forming a climate change club might have been after-school endeavors only. But this can limit the scope of the learning and work. If a school moves a service club from the after-school context, where the group might meet for a few hours at most each month, that group and its mission suddenly are accorded several hours each week and given the benefit of a dedicated teacher and other resources to get their work done.

Granted, the after-school space is often a safer space in which teachers and kids can get political. People are opting in, rather than required to be there. This is where service clubs often thrive. But the increased safety is exchanged for less time and fewer students with access. Taking the after-school pursuits and passions of teachers and students and integrating them into school-day hours gives schools the opportunity to engage more students and provides greater capacity and obligation to go deeper, to expand the intellectual and political dimensions of the work and learning.

And a school needs all the time it can afford to get political, carefully and deliberately, which is how we must proceed in a time when our society is so polarized and there is so much risk of misunderstanding and personal attack.

CROSS-POLLINATION, OR CLASH OF CIVILIZATIONS?

Our children are growing up in an era characterized both by strengthening divisions and the mixing of peoples, an era of both mass-migration and the fortification of borders, a period of both self-absorption and the easy exposure to difference. Parents, youth, and people of all ages seek certainty and stability in times of change.

Seeking certainty, many of us will retreat from difference, from the challenging of assumptions, from debate. We will instead find stability in the mirroring of ourselves and our ideas in others that look and sound like us. This is a normal mode in adolescence, and it is to be expected in the broader society. We hear it in our debates about immigration, borders, and walls. Where some might see a melting pot of peoples and the healthy cross-pollination of ideas, others will see a clash of civilizations.

U.S. President Donald Trump gave a speech in Poland in 2017 that painted a picture of such a clash. The president wondered whether Western civilization had the "will to survive." He offered only a vague description of the enemies to that survival, but he gave enough precision for the image of danger to take shape. He talked of borders and worried about external threats coming from the "South or the East." He lauded a Western civilization defined by common culture, traditions, and faith: a civilization that writes "symphonies," values works of art that "honor God," and worships common "ancient heroes." He declared that "our civilization, and our survival depend on these bonds of history, culture, and memory."[16]

Trump also named free speech and free expression as essential elements of this civilization, which is good to hear a president affirm. But he drew boundaries around the lineage of our civilization in ways that exclude the expressions, stories, and identities of many U.S. citizens, families, and students. One can easily imagine calls to narrow the curriculum in the wake of remarks like this.

The pulpit of the president has a kind of prophetic power, the power to prompt and sanction. Trump's remarks about violence against protestors at his campaign rallies preceded violence against protesters at his rallies: in February 2016, he told supporters to "knock the crap out of" protesters, and in March 2016 one of his supporters punched a man in the face as he was being escorted out of a rally. Likewise, Trump's violent rhetoric against journalists coincided with violence against journalists: in 2015 he joked about killing journalists, and continued to deride journalists as a routine element of his campaign for president; later, as president, he would speak admiringly of a congressional candidate in Montana who assaulted a reporter asking a question about healthcare.

In similar fashion, Trump's ethnocentric musings on what music, art, and stories comprise the essence of Western civilization may foreshadow calls to narrow what is permitted as the content of teaching and learning in our schools. Not to say that narrowing and silencing is unfamiliar to school communities across our country, past and present. The 2010 law banning Mexican American studies in Arizona is a disheartening example—even while the resistance to that law is inspiring.

So this is a difficult time to be a teacher who tries to value the various identities and histories that walk into our classrooms each day, which makes it a difficult time to put learning in a political context. A veteran Vermont teacher remarked in 2017 that for the first time in seventeen years she'd been accused of proffering a liberal agenda. She was engaging her students in a letter-writing project she'd done in similar fashion many times before. Some concerned parents were troubled by what they saw as a liberal political agenda, while others thought she was simply fostering discussion of how to change the world for the better. Perhaps both statements are true.

Should this teacher have sanitized her curriculum of topics about which she felt passionate? Were the voices criticizing her being inappropriately intolerant of political content in the classroom, or were they being appropriately vigilant about the risks of indoctrination? Is school a place for political debate and contemporary problem solving?

The answer to the last question is yes. *Yes*, school is a place for political debate and contemporary problem solving. *But* we need to do this in a way that minimizes the risk for misunderstanding and personal attack.

RISK

In the spring of 2017 Principal Gilman got a call from a parent, Mr. Hoyt. He wasn't yelling, but his tone, and how his voice caught in his throat, conveyed strong emotion. He was angry that the school had forced his son to participate in a rally calling for action on global warming. There were images of the rally online and in the papers. What if his son's face appeared in those pictures?

Mr. Hoyt was concerned about teacher bias and the imposition of an ideology other than his own. There are two sides to the climate change story, he asserted. He said this several times. Mr. Gilman was surprised by the call, for he'd known the student for several years and this was the first time he'd ever heard from the father. Mr. Gilman affirmed the importance of the father's concerns, and said he would look into it.

After talking to the teacher, Mr. Gilman could see that yes, in one sense, they had made his son participate in the rally. Attending the demonstration was fieldwork for a class; permission forms had gone home and been signed. It was a documentary film class, and the students were learning about how to use their cameras, how to conduct interviews, how to capture live action.

They were attending the march as documentarians, not to protest or affirm any one side of the story. Mr. Gilman asked the teacher to call Mr. Hoyt and discuss this with him. She did, and it helped. This is an example of how, in today's political climate, more than the normal dose of preparation may be needed when doing work that involves politically charged topics—and a reminder that our schools must not shy away from the task.

The core purpose of public schools is to help young people become able contributors to our society, informed and critical-thinking citizens in our democracy. Topics of potent political and personal relevance must be the stuff of the curriculum. And the role of schools in this regard is as important today as ever. Public schools are among the few public settings where the adults, by the very nature of their vocation, must have high expectations for evidence-based and respectful dialogue. Other public servants—to say nothing of our newscasters and entertainers—may be able to fool themselves in thinking they're still doing their job when they make fact-flimsy proclamations, or flaunt the norms of civil discourse, or pander to people's fears. Teachers must never succumb to this.

It isn't easy, though. It is difficult to facilitate mature discussions of complex issues with so little modeling of it in the mainstream culture. And there is risk for teachers who engage other people's children in activities that bring about strong beliefs and ideological divisions. Feelings can get hurt. Students can feel that their values are being challenged—and perhaps they are. Teachers will sometimes be accused of bias or indoctrination. But our democracy desperately needs diverse voices to engage in mature dialogue if we are to ever find compassionate solutions to our common problems—and schools must be where young citizens learn to do this.

So how can teachers open the door to controversial topics—like climate change, or police brutality, or gun rights, or war in the Middle East—without being vulnerable to accusations of pushing a political agenda? How can we embrace the plurality of identity that walks into our schools each day, and turn this diversity into opportunities for learning?

Granted, not all school populations reflect the diversity of the broader society. Some of our neighborhoods and schools are deeply segregated by race and socioeconomic status. But many of our schools are microcosms of the vast diversity of our country, and even those that look homogeneous by one measure are, when we look below the surface, heterogeneous in other ways. Even in the average, mostly white, central Vermont school, like Mr. Gilman's, the list of minority demographic groups is long—Native American, black, Latino, Asian—even though the actual number of minority students is low. And within the white majority itself, one often finds a variety of religious, socioeconomic, and professional family backgrounds.

Wherever we teach, we are teaching in a place of many identities, and we need to find ways to safely situate teaching and learning in personal and political contexts. How can we fortify our classrooms so that they can get political and be the strong containers of civic work and civil discourse that our democracy so desperately needs them to be? Here are four priorities to keep in mind:

1. Experiences that value every family
2. Reverence for discussion and debate
3. Multiple (community-sourced) perspectives
4. Homework as fieldwork: inform by engaging

GET POLITICAL: FOUR PRIORITIES

1. Experiences that Value Every Family

The Get Personal classroom and the Get Political classroom are inherently linked. The foundation for getting political is curriculum and pedagogy that builds personal trust among and with students and their families. One way to do this is through lessons, activities, and projects that value family identities and stories.

Whether they come from conservative or liberal families, it is important that all students feel they were born into a home and history that has worth. Teachers can establish trust with students and families by explicitly exploring and valuing elements of what each child calls home and family.

At the school where Mr. Hoyt sent his child and where Mr. Gilman was principal, "Where I'm From" poems adorn the walls of eighth-grade classrooms every fall. Mr. Gilman takes pictures of those poems each year, focusing in close on specific words and phrases. He puts them in slide shows for assemblies and for the eighth-grade graduation, evoking the images and stories of the places these children call home: the gardens, the closets, the pictures on the walls, the aromas of a grandmother's cooking, the rough wool of grandfather's winter pants, the dirt bikes and chainsaws, the deer camp and farm house, the fears and losses and songs. The "Where I'm From" words and phrases settle on the screen amid pictures of student artwork: paintings of faces, still-life sketches, green and blue landscapes of the hills where the children grew up, and fanciful representations of other worlds the children may imagine.

In that same eighth-grade graduation ceremony, every student proceeds across the stage to offer a "This I Believe" statement. For most students this is the largest audience they've ever spoken to, but they conquer their fears and every student's voice sounds in an auditorium packed with families. The school is affirming that every child holds dear a belief that the school would like to hear. At the end of this ceremony each student is given a gift, including a card with a personal note from a teacher, and a flower. The students are invited to give the flower to a friend or family member who has supported them in their growing up.

Other important ingredients of the middle school experience likewise help build trust, value each child and family, and lay the foundation for work that gets political. Social studies and English classes culminate in an extensive interdisciplinary local history project, which engages every student in the study of a local landmark, historical event, or family history. Some of the best projects are done by students who probe the past of their own families: a grandfather who fought in Vietnam, a great-grandmother who kept diaries, a farm passed down through generations. Simple as they may be in concept, these are projects and assignments that help each family feel valued. They build trust, and lay a foundation that schools need when shifting toward work that challenges assumptions and puts politics on the table and identity on the agenda.

Mr. Hoyt's son had participated in these middle school experiences in seventh and eighth grade. This may be why he chose to call and talk, rather than display his frustration on Facebook or silently resent what had happened. He reached out and confronted the school with his concerns. The work that the middle school teachers did with this student and family over the years helped shape this father's willingness to engage in the debate.

2. Reverence for Discussion and Debate

If our relationships with families are solid, then we are in a stronger place to engage our pupils in learning from difference, ideological dissonance, and—in the right measure—from some degree of emotional discomfort. Key containers for this dissonance and discomfort are dialogue, discussion, and debate. The Get Political classroom needs a lot of time for talking.

Teachers and administrators must hold dialogue and debate in high regard. With popular political discourse as ugly as it is, debates about ideas can quickly devolve into put-downs. Controversial speakers are often not allowed to speak, even at our most liberal academic institutions. In such a context, it is challenging for a teacher to bring contemporary topics to the syllabus. Teachers need to know that administrators will support them if and when challenges arise.

Administrators who are ready for this work should tell every new teacher that the school welcomes calls from families about a political topic or identity question raised in the classroom. Such calls are a sign that kids are talking about their studies at home, and a sign that teachers are challenging students to think about serious issues. And it's good for our democracy.

When we don't encourage kids to take a critical look at themselves and their society, we are reinforcing—implicitly, and therefore powerfully—the political and economic status quo. That may be what certain forces in society want, but it is not what a just society needs. It's not what youth or communities need, either. We don't want the destructive forces of adolescence seeking their outlet in the shape of a bloody event, some blade or bullet turned inward on the self or outward on others. Better we let them do battle with their beliefs—constructively—and in this way come to know their power and purpose in the world. Administrators must be willing to explain this to any parent or community member who might dispute the notion that our classrooms should tackle issues with ethical and political dimensions. That said, we can only defend this if we do it well.

Part of doing this kind of teaching well is being dedicated to the whole class discussion. Again, there is overlap here with the Get Personal classroom. The classroom that gets political also requires norms and guidelines for approaching charged topics through discussion. These discussions need to carefully balance safety and trust with risk-taking and discomfort. In addition to the norms named in the previous chapter—*avoid absolutes*, *one mic*, and *I statements*—here is another norm for conversations that can be emotionally charged: *Disagree with the idea, not the person.* When hosting conversations about challenging topics, no one should feel personally attacked. Removing names from disagreements is useful in this regard. When students hold contrasting ideas or beliefs, we can phrase our statements in such a way that we are talking about the person's idea, not the person himself. For example, it's better to say, "I disagree with the idea that abortion is morally wrong because . . . " instead of saying "I disagree with Jorge that abortion is morally wrong." This helps keep sensitive adolescents from feeling devalued by name. Even if the debate is vigorous, students will be less likely to have negative feelings about the discussion if this norm is followed.

In addition to establishing norms, there are many in-the-moment decisions a teacher can make to cultivate healthy discussions about complicated topics. Here is a menu of strategies for teachers to help cultivate healthy and dynamic discussions:

• *Make it moral:* Engage yourself and others by giving questions, comments, and topics a moral or ethical context. In posing questions, use words like "good" and "bad" and "right" and "wrong." Use words like "fair" and "unfair." Every topic has a moral/ethical dimension. This is inherently engaging for people because our moral sense connects so deeply to our sense of ourselves as good people.

• *Affirm and require questions:* Show enthusiasm for the topic, and especially show enthusiasm for questions. Don't just begin discussions with questions; end discussions with questions—about even the most minor things. Require questions. Even the most superficial questions require students to stop and self-reflect. For example, state "I know you may think we've covered everything, but before we end this discussion and move on, the class has to ask three questions."

- *Be the devil's advocate:* Engender debate and controversy. Even if you agree, pose the opposing viewpoint—and feel free to be transparent that you are doing so, and why.
- *Make connections:* We can do this simply by keeping track of and noting commonalities and disagreements between the views expressed by students. For example, use phrases such as "I noticed, Ted, when you spoke, that you seem to be saying . . . Which reminds me of what Sylvia just said . . . But I bet, Rondell, that you would disagree this idea, because you were saying the opposite; is that right?" In such fashion students begin to see how their ideas connect to and can build on each other.
- *Coax:* For those students having difficulty jumping in, encourage them to agree or disagree, and tell them that a positive and valid contribution to the discussion can simply be a statement of whether they agree or disagree with someone else's point. They can restate an idea as long as they do it in their own, new words. For students who have little experience speaking confidently in public, this is a lower-stakes way to gain some experience.
- *Give advance notice:* Warn students who are hesitant to speak that you will be asking to hear their voice in a few moments, and tell them in advance what kinds of comments they might make. Or tell the class that after a few more speakers you plan to do a go-round to hear from people who have not yet spoken.
- *Paraphrase:* You can check for understanding, validate someone's ideas, affirm that you are listening, or elaborate on an idea—all simply by paraphrasing. The teacher can paraphrase student ideas, and can ask students to paraphrase for each other. This is another easy way to enable a student to contribute who may not be willing to share his or her own ideas yet, or to check for listening if someone seems distracted.
- *Delegate:* As noted above, the teacher can ask a student to paraphrase the idea of another student, rather than the teacher doing this herself. The teacher can also delegate to students the job of re-stating a question, re-reading a passage, or clarifying something.
- *Delegate more:* After modeling how to lead a discussion, allow students to do it; for example, ask students to keep a speakers list, lead a protocol, or call on participants, including you as the teacher.
- *Remain in control:* Even though students can facilitate many aspects of a discussion, you should always take power back or break protocol when necessary—simply be transparent about why you are doing it. This is especially important if a sensitive topic is being approached, or if a reprimand is appropriate, or if boundaries need to be clarified. Be very firm about such boundaries when needed. If a sensitive topic is on the horizon,

interrupt to suggest parameters for talking or not talking about it. If a
student violates a norm or rule with disrespectful talk, interrupt to stop it.

- *Model everything:* Model what you want your students to do, and do it
self-consciously and transparently. For example, say "Now, I'm modeling
the way that you can disagree with someone's idea." And highlight when
students have just offered good models; for example state, "Now, Theresa
just did a good job of substantiating her idea with evidence from . . . "

- *Whisper:* Use the unstructured moments before and after a discussion to
connect individually and privately with students: inform them of the discussion topics or questions to come, encourage them to share ideas and
thoughts, remind them of points they might make or questions and ideas
they previously expressed, congratulate them on a good contribution, or
follow up with a response to something they said. Also use these aside
moments to talk to your student leaders or potential leaders to tell them
how they can help others in the upcoming discussion and what you hope
to hear from them.

- *Love their mistakes:* Always find something to praise or affirm—including a mistake or question—and do it as part of your efforts to point out
faults and flaws in their arguments. For instance, you might say "I love
that you are taking the risk to share that idea, but you missed one important thing . . . "

- *Debrief:* Take time to reflect on the discussion and remark on what was
good about it and what can be improved. In the whole class setting, it is
best to generally emphasize what worked well more than what did not.
The repeated emphasis on and modeling of good practice will positively
reinforce expectations and gradually reduce what's not working.

Because the popular culture offers so few models of respectful discussion
and intellectual debate, it is important that all members of a school community—especially the adults—be skilled at modeling and engaging each other
in respectful talk and listening. Every teacher should try to articulate for
himself what a good discussion looks like and use that understanding to
shape norms, build assessment rubrics, and convey expectations to students
and families. That said, there's no reason to reinvent the wheel—or the
circle—when it comes to structuring and facilitating a discussion.

Protocols, debate formats, Socratic seminars, mock trials, circle processes: careful facilitation guidelines and compelling formats of all kinds are
readily available off the shelf or internet for teachers to use in the classroom.
In a 2015 post on the website "Cult of Pedagogy," Jennifer Gonzalez com-
piles fifteen different approaches to structuring discussions, categorizing
them into those that require greater or lesser degrees of advance preparation.
Gonzalez notes in the opening of her post that, when mentoring new teachers, she would often hear them say "we will discuss . . . " as a strategy to use

in a lesson, which, without adequate preparation, risks being very unlike whole class discussion:

> I was pretty sure that *We will discuss* actually meant the teacher would do most of the talking; He would throw out a couple of questions like "So what did you think about the video?" or "What was the theme of the story?" and a few students would respond, resulting in something that *looked* like a discussion, but was ultimately just a conversation between the teacher and a handful of extroverted students.[17]

Sometimes an abundance of structure is a very good thing for a discussion that gets political. It gives students and the teacher rules to play by, such that multiple voices are heard in careful fashion, and it adds transparency regarding how the positional power of the teacher is being used. The more clear we are about the care with which we approach sensitive topics, the better able we are to defend our practice when it is questioned by parents and others who are wary of indoctrination, or who believe that kids cannot handle heavy topics—or worse, who are unable to recognize the various dangers inherent when youth sit in silence.

3. Multiple (Community-Sourced) Perspectives

Reverence for discussion rings loud and clear in an important book, *The Political Classroom*, by Diana E. Hess and Paula McAvoy. This book is good resource for teachers, administrators, and the teachers of teachers who believe that schools "are charged with preparing young people for life in a democracy."[18] Ethical questions, philosophical considerations—and the practical implications of both—are explored with sensitivity to the diversity of our student population and with tender awareness of the personal and professional dilemmas that teachers face when approaching political topics in the classroom.

Hess and McAvoy present several studies of classrooms in which political topics were intentionally approached, with various methodologies and degrees of effectiveness. One of their findings is that there is evidence both for and against teachers sharing their own political leanings with a class of students. They write, "we have concluded that teachers ought to think about disclosing and withholding their political views as pedagogical tools that should be used intentionally and with good judgment."[19] In determining how to exercise this judgment, the authors show that much depends on the sociopolitical community the school is part of, the homogeneity or heterogeneity of the class, the pedagogy of the teacher, and teacher tact.

A teacher can responsibly share his or her beliefs about a topic, or a teacher can keep those views private. Both can be effective. Above all, it is schoolhouse silence about matters of contemporary political relevance that should concern us. It is the duty of the teacher to empower children to answer questions for themselves, and the duty of the teacher to expose the child to multiple perspectives on any topic. If, in so doing, a child is exposed to the political leanings of a teacher, better that than the more insidious exposure to unspoken bias, the subtleties of micro-aggressions, and the damage that silence can do when passively sanctioning injustice.

It is an illusion that neutrality is neutral, and we should not strive for it as an end in itself. Nor can we ever account for all of the various sides of a story that any political topic might have. But we can strive for balance, and we can make sure that there are multiple, credibly sourced perspectives that inform a student's exploration of a contemporary topic or challenge.

A particularly powerful and credible way to expose students to a variety of viewpoints is to bring into the classroom community members with expertise on a given topic. Having an array of community leaders with informed opinions participate in a project is one way of buttressing the teacher's efforts with the strength of local professionals and leaders. This creates allies in the community who feel invested and who can affirm the integrity of their work in the face of any concern that the school might be inappropriately exposing a child to political beliefs not supported in the home.

Teachers who offer electives in the PBL Lab mentioned above are required to forge community partnerships as part of their approach to contemporary challenges. The Restorative Justice elective opened the year with a training by the local Restorative Justice board, which brought into the class the director of that organization, another community member, and a local police officer. The Interact service-learning elective has collaborated routinely with members of the local Rotary Club, which includes powerful leaders from business and municipal government. A Climate Change elective collaborated with the local state college, shared student learning at a local café, and culminated in presentations that engaged state congressional representatives.

In the Get to Work chapter that follows, there will be further discussion of connecting to community and forging curriculum partnerships. Just as there is overlap between the Get Personal and Get Political classroom, there is much that Get Political has in common with Get to Work.

4. Homework as Fieldwork: Inform by Engaging

A key benefit of community engagement is that community members who are engaged in teaching and learning become informed conveyors of information about what is happening in the school. They tell their spouses, colleagues, and friends. Information spreads, and the mystery of what sometimes happens in school dissipates. This is crucial. When the stakes are high, a little bit of information can go a long way toward allaying concerns born of uncertainty. And the stakes—hard-earned tax dollars, people's children, the future workforce—are certainly high when it comes to a community's schools.

Engaging families to the right degree in what happens in the classroom should be as much of a priority as engaging community members. Elizabeth Kleinrock, a third-grade teacher and recipient of a Teaching Tolerance Award for Excellence, writes about seeing families as partners—and not allowing "fear of parent pushback" from preventing "us from engaging in conversations around social justice issues." She writes, "We should work to have open lines of communication and engage with families in ways that support student learning and growth."[20] She offers several strategies for doing this, including "Give Families a Heads-Up":

> Families do not like being blindsided, especially when it comes to their children. Before starting a unit that could be considered "divisive," I alert families to upcoming lessons or conversations and then follow up to let them know how things went. (This is not the same as asking for permission, which implies that discussing inclusivity and difference is wrong.)[21]

Indeed, students' homes can be turned into centers of support through engagement and information sharing. Engaging families is a means of informing families.

Teachers do not need to routinely give opt-out opportunities to kids and parents, but we should ensure that families know the standards, the research, the credible sources, and the rationale for the work in which we are engaging the community's children. However, simply sharing information in a syllabus or a form letter only goes so far, and is a one-way communication means with not much room for meaningful response. Instead, we can find ways to share information by including families in the work. Even a very simple task can help ensure there are no big surprises, and can even allow voices from the home to become part of the conversation.

Reflecting back on the experience of Mr. Hoyt, his son, and the class that attended the climate march as documentarians, one can imagine a simple task given to students in preparation for their fieldwork: "Ask three adults in your life outside of school for their opinions on how climate change is covered in the media. What do they hear? What do they believe?" A simple homework task thus becomes fieldwork, part of the class's exploration of the topic. Meanwhile, families are simultaneously engaged in the work, having their own voices solicited and valued, and learning something important about what students are studying.

Engagement of this kind helps manage anxiety and fear. In the current polarized political climate, teachers who bring topics of personal and political relevance into the classroom are likely to make some students and families uncomfortable. This can lead to conflict, and teachers are vulnerable to accusations of bias.

Teachers may be tempted to shy away from controversial and emotional content. But helping young people become critically thinking citizens in our democracy is a core purpose of schooling that we must not abandon—and it sometimes entails learning experiences that challenge beliefs and assumptions. We can strengthen our classrooms to carry this heavy responsibility by building a foundation of engagement, transparency, and trust with families and community members.

MISPLACED FEARS

Before concluding this chapter, it is important to note that another significant barrier to getting political in the classroom is far more internal: an educator's own misplaced fears about what kids can handle, and our misperceptions of what constitutes "relevance." Educators must reframe how we think about children's capacity for engaging in heavy topics, and we must also reframe how we conceive of relevance.

The worry about whether a child can handle a weighty topic is a sentiment not uncommon to many of us—both as parents and teachers. But more than young people, adults are the ones likely to become overwhelmed by big problems and default to complacency, cynicism, or silence. In interviews conducted by Hesse and McAvoy after students completed courses that explored charged political content, and in interviews conducted years later, students affirmed the value of these courses. This was true even when students found the topics personally challenging, or when they found the views of peers difficult or offensive to hear. Hess and McAvoy conclude:

> Even though we encountered many examples of discussions that were extremely difficult for some students, in the literally hundreds of interviews we did while students were in class and in the follow-up calls after study participants had left high school, very few students thought it would be wise to strip the curriculum of such issues. Notably, what clearly emerged was students' view that the curriculum ought to include these issues.[22]

When appropriately exposed to topics of even the most colossal implications—mortality, death, racism, sexuality, war, oppression—kids typically engage with varying degrees of curiosity, daring, and idealism. For adolescents especially, finding strong identity anchors through strong expressions of belief is something they need. One of the most compelling rationales for a curriculum that gets political is that it can help young people access the ideological commitments and statements of belief that help them feel like somebody. The question "Who am I?" which can echo like so much emptiness during adolescence, can be answered powerfully with statements of "I believe."

REFRAMING RELEVANCE

How educators think about "relevance" also needs to be reframed. There are many teachers—from the progressive constructivist to the traditional "sage on the stage"—who equate curriculum relevance with student "interest," what kids are "into," what they "like to do." Such a conception of relevance is indeed an important starting point.

As Christopher Emdin instructively illustrates in *For White Folks Who Teach in the Hood . . . and the Rest of Y'all, Too*, a teacher should use student interests and the cultural contexts of their lives as a key to opening the door to a relationship with these students, to lay the foundation of trust on which student engagement is built. Such efforts are especially important when the doors to those relationships are closed with the locks and legacies of racial and socioeconomic division. Across such chasms, when teachers validate the fashion, music, foods—and the activities students do for fun when they feel free to be themselves—it can help students feel that they are being seen and understood by the teacher. It "allows the teacher to circumvent the tensions that come from the cultural misalignments between school and community."[23]

In fact, Emdin's wise guidance pushes the teacher much further than circumventing tensions. He offers pathways for educators to connect even more deeply to the cultural contexts and identity strengths of the students they work with, from the modes of expression in popular song and religious traditions, to the architectural shapes and artifacts of the places where they live. The results are classrooms in which students feel seen and valued, and lessons in which students are excited and engaged: "When a teacher makes connections between context [of the students' lives] and content, innovative lessons that connect things like graffiti and mathematics or hip-hop music and science begin to emerge."[24]

An especially deep level of relevance can be achieved when we augment our notion of relevance based on student "interest" with the concept of relevance derived from "need." What are the developmental needs of young people? What are the basic needs of their families? What are the social and economic needs of the broader community in which they and we live? Asking these questions pushes the curriculum into regions more profound than interest, which can be fleeting.

Reframing relevance in terms of need takes us to topics and questions like those named in the courses listed early in this chapter: Is it too late for meaningful action on climate change? Does a school suspension have any connection to dropping out? Do our schools and courts treat people fairly? How does racism operate to place some in power and others on the outskirts? What are the most important labor struggles in U.S. history? How open should our borders be? What is the history of LGBT individuals in the broader narrative of American history? What are the diplomatic issues and international systems that lend themselves to fostering war and peace?

COURAGEOUS CURRICULUM CONTENT

Jeremiah who swaggers, Roberto who stumbles, Jenny who tells her stories in scars, the boys who contemplate grim violence toward their peers—each of these children, and all the others in less extreme emotional states, need schools that offer them courageous curriculum content: classrooms that are spaces where ideals, values, and traditions are surfaced and confronted; bold and sensitive lessons and projects that allow for the honest exposure of individual and societal histories.

Our students need to see their lives in political and historical context, to have the adults in their world honor the urgency of the present, and to discover hope in looking toward the future. They need classrooms with topic questions that offer up the past for a deep re-examination, explorations that yield both pride and outrage, that catalyze in young people both the impulse to preserve and the impetus to correct for the future—on a personal and societal level.

In classrooms that embody these imperatives we find wise and skilled inquiry-based instruction through which teachers reveal students' assumptions and past experience as the first step to building new knowledge. The political and personal intertwine. In such classrooms one will witness teachers loving their work because their own personal values and political passions inform it.

These are teachers attuned and bold enough to craft lessons that make the students' familial and childhood pasts become present in the classroom: the beauty of that past, the pains, the achievements, the dignity, the wrongs. These teachers turn the same attention to our country, the United States. They ask the big questions, questions that expose the dreadful, comic, tragic, and glorious. The guiding questions of their projects and conversations lead their students—through exploration of self and society—to condemn societal ills but also to marvel at what is beautiful and revere what is good.

And the horizon at the end of the course will always be another question about what's next and how to do future good as best we can. For no curriculum potent with the exploration of ideals and our personal and collective pasts should have the shimmer of its horizon obstructed by the dull wall of only an exam. Comprehensive exams have their place. But if our only answer to "why?" is "to pass the test," then we are breaking the heart of youth. There are more legitimate causes, more powerful dreams to see as reasons for the work.

QUESTIONS FOR REFLECTION AND DISCUSSION

1. The course descriptions shared in this chapter, from both private and public schools, have content that is expressly political. Are there courses like these in the schools you know? If not, should there be? If yes, are they positive learning experiences for students? Why or why not?
2. Research cited in this chapter suggests that it can be effective when teachers do not reveal their own political leanings, and that it can also be effective when teachers are transparent about their positions. Which do you think is the best approach?
3. This chapter argues that an especially deep level of relevance can be achieved when we derive curriculum topics from "need" rather than "interest." In your community, what are the basic needs of youth and their families? What are the social and economic needs of the broader community? How can curriculum content be derived from such needs?
4. Do any of the four guidelines for the Get Political classroom seem appropriate to implement in your school context? Why or why not? What benefits might there be? What concerns?

Chapter Seven

GET TO WORK

The notion that "applied" knowledge is somehow less worthy than "pure" knowledge was natural to a society in which all useful work was performed by slaves and serfs.

—John Dewey[1]

Young adults are just that: people on the starting line of adulthood. They have many years of able adulthood ahead of them, including all their remaining years of formal schooling. A community is missing out on a huge opportunity when it insulates the early years of able adulthood from engagement in adult thinking and adult tasks.

If we consider late adulthood to begin around age sixty-five, and young adulthood to begin around fifteen years of age, that gives us about fifty years of early-to-middle adulthood when the body and mind are particularly able to engage in work that the community needs doing. For most people who graduate and go on to post-secondary school settings, high school and time in college comprise five or more years—or about 10 percent of adulthood. Why would we allow 10 percent of our most able years of adulthood to be insulated from political inquiry, contemporary problem solving, and meaningful work? Child labor laws have their place, but schools can do much more to put kids to work solving the problems our world needs to solve. The students are ready.

In 2016, First Lady Michelle Obama delivered what have been called some of the most powerful speeches of the 2016 presidential election. Her October speech in New Hampshire, just weeks before election day, enthralled and moved millions. Why?

111

In part what makes Michelle Obama such a powerful speaker is that she gets personal, then she gets political, and then she demands we get to work in the service of our ideals.

Early in her New Hampshire address, she shifted her tone from rousing to grave and tells her audience, "I'm going to get a little serious here, because I think we can all agree that this has been a rough week in an already rough election. This week has been particularly interesting for me personally . . ." She talks about the personal impact that Donald Trump's remarks about sexually assaulting women have had on her, as a woman, as a parent, as a citizen. She gets personal: "I have to tell you that I can't stop thinking about this. It has shaken me to my core in a way that I couldn't have predicted." And she keeps it personal, reflecting on what it is like to hear degrading remarks, and reflecting on the men she knows who do not treat women in such ways. She soon shifted from the personal to the political, the national election and its implications. And then she demands her supporters get to work—that the women she is speaking to, in particular, get to work: "We have knowledge. We have a voice. We have a vote." She tells her audience to get to work: "[W]e can't just sit around wringing our hands. Now, we need to recover from our shock and depression and do what women have always done in this country. We need you to roll up your sleeves. We need to get to work."[2]

Some have called this a "speech for the ages." It is certainly a speech to keep in mind as we think about schooling that engages young people and the kind of imperatives that must inform curriculum reform in schools.

GET TO WORK

That crucial question of adolescence—"Who am I?"—can be answered, as we have noted, with idealism and statements of "I believe." With just as much power, young people can answer that question with statements of "I can do." This is the importance of a curriculum that puts young people to work. The reflections of Erik Erikson continue to provide guidance here. In his stages of identity development, one of the dualities he locates in early adolescence is that of industry versus inferiority, which, when negotiated effectively, results in a feeling of competence, of doing something well.[3]

Picture a middle school STEM class, an interdisciplinary science-technology-engineering-mathematics class in which the students are getting to work. The shop is a retrofitted common classroom, but traditional tools are everywhere and the industry/inferiority duality of the young adolescents is vividly displayed. The students are accessing their industriousness—their need and ability to build and to do—under the guidance of a wise teacher.

The teacher is paying equal attention, in his learning intentions and class discussions, to their industriousness and to the students' tendency to feel inferior in the eyes of others. The teacher helps them see that this is a learning experience that requires trial and error, success and failure. They are building hydraulic arms from simple kits. They are in teams, some struggling, some not. They are wrestling with how to secure with clamps, where to place the gears, whose idea to try next, what help to ask from the teacher. Afterward, they will discuss as a class, and write short journal entries. "What was the best mistake you made today?" he asks. He conveys to them that making mistakes is problem solving, not a problem in itself.

Feeling inferior is a strong proclivity in adolescence. But a good teacher can turn failed attempts away from feelings of shame, away from the student's instinct to situate the self in a status hierarchy, and toward logical steps in a creative process. Normalizing and learning from failure is the way to get competent at something.

The capacity for competence at using adult tools to execute important tasks only continues to grow as the young person's body and intellect grow in strength and dexterity. And so it's our responsibility to provide young people with opportunities to use tools of the adult world to approach adult tasks. When you walk into a classroom or school that understands this, you hear it in the language that teachers are using: They talk to students in math and science classes as if they are young mathematicians, technicians, engineers, architects, or designers. The social studies teacher talks to students about doing the work of actual historians, economists, or journalists. The curriculum is often project-based, and the most compelling projects correlate to something the community needs to be done. As a result, children feel valued.

With child labor prohibitions and the length of childhood dependency so prolonged in our country, sitting in our schools every day we have a massive untapped labor force. Why not set the kids to work on tasks that our schools and towns need doing? John Dewey, in the epigraph at the start of this chapter, reminds us of one reason why not.

There is a class consciousness and bias that informs our reluctance to bring the curriculum out of the ivory tower and into the world of work. Perhaps the dominant culture values less our applied, hands-on, vocational or technical programs because once upon a time it was a dehumanized class of serfs and slaves that got their hands dirty, while the more privileged hands exercised their intellect in a realm more seemingly clean and superior. Obviously this hierarchy is not a mere relic of the past. Blue-collar and white-collar learning tracks are certainly tangible in our schools today. And these tracks track all of us. We get stuck.

THE ABSTRACTION-APPLICATION GAP

As has been noted, in many rural communities across the country, adults matter-of-factly teach young people how to hunt with guns, and in every region of the nation adults teach kids how to drive cars. With a combination of individual mentorship, group lessons, some reading and writing and practical application, adults mentor students in how to use these powerful tools to complete adult tasks and meet real-world needs. The stakes are often high—food for the family, transportation to work, developmental rites of passage, family traditions—and people can die when the tools are wielded incorrectly.

Driving and hunting are two remarkably commonplace invitations to young people to wield adult tools for heavy practical tasks, and this ought to inspire us to see what is possible in other domains. For the same can be true of calculus and biology. The same can be true of history, psychology, sociology, and economics. The stakes can be high in these areas too, and it is the teacher's job to help illuminate where the urgency lies, helping students find those opportunities for application when a young person's impatience to apply the tool or concept is palpable and the need is pressing. Unfortunately, many teachers do not have the training or experience that lends itself to curriculum that gets to work.

Many of us who have become high school teachers do so in part because we were once very comfortable in high school classrooms. This is a fine recipe for perpetuating the kind of schooling that divorces knowledge, theory, and abstraction from work and application outside the classroom. Familiar is the story of the English teacher who did well in English classes in high school. He or she then attends college classrooms and declares an English major. This young professional then leaves college and becomes a high school English teacher. What experience other than sitting in English class can this person bring to bear upon the work of being a teacher? What professionals did this person ever work with other than teachers and professors? Very rarely in most people's tenure as student or teacher does a person ever encounter any incentive or expectation to collaborate with citizens who work in fields related to the subject of study.

Principals and hiring committees with a different vision of what schooling entails—a vision in which the curriculum gets to work—would be right to be wary of hiring people who follow the traditional pathway to teacherhood.

When applicants say in a hiring interview that they decided to become a teacher of their subject because they always loved that subject as a student, this should give us pause. It's not that we don't want teachers to have a long-standing love of their discipline and the classroom; the concern is that if teachers are the only professionals that a teacher has ever worked with, this teacher may not have enough experience in other sectors of society to push school curriculum to get to work. That said, schools can support a teacher's professional growth in this area. And school leaders must realize that without the right incentives and supports, it isn't actually fair to expect traditional English, math, science, and social studies teachers to extensively collaborate with professionals outside the school.

There's only so much collaboration with professionals in other sectors that we can reasonably expect of high school teachers. Teaching is an inherently collaborative and interactive endeavor. Consider a high school teacher who has eighty students across her classes. This teacher—who has a student load lower than many—is already collaborating with a lot of students and families. If we add in communication with colleagues, then he has even more interactions in a given week: thousands of interactions, and they all can feel high-stakes when working with kids.

Teaching is among one of the few occupations in which a person is asked daily to have interpersonal interactions in this quantity and at such a high level of importance to the community. So it is a tall order, on top of this work, to ask teachers to collaborate—meaningfully and regularly—with other professionals outside the school. But this is where we need to go if young people are to see their work and themselves as important to the world they live in. And so we need to design the necessary supports. Those supports include schedules that lessen the number of curricula and children a particular teacher must engage in a week; administrative support for relationship-building with citizens outside the school; and professional development in project-based learning pedagogies.

Shifting our resources in these directions, however, first requires a mind-set shift. Just as we need to reframe how we conceive of "relevance," conceptual adjustments are needed to help dismantle in our own minds the false dichotomy between "school" on the one hand and "real world" on the other. Closing the abstraction-application gap starts with the language we use and how we conceive of schooling. There are several mind-set shifts we can prioritize as educators to help us better articulate and design curriculum that gets to work:

1. From service to citizenship
2. From guest to partner
3. From fieldtrip to fieldwork
4. From audience to consumer

GET TO WORK: FOUR PRIORITIES

1. From Service to Citizenship

"Service learning" connotes learning and work that serve others or the greater good in some way. These are laudable ends. But too often the very concept of service learning isolates service in a particular project, club, or checklist of hours to be logged. Isolating service in this way can convey the idea that the rest of what we do is somehow not in the service of the greater good, thus maintaining a problematic separation of the ivory tower and the street. It is better that we conceive of citizenship—not service—as the broader imperative for what we do.

This is not to suggest service learning and community service don't have their place. These are common ways schools currently put students to work in settings outside the school. These after-school, weekend, or extracurricular activities are often positive experiences for those involved. But there's a risk that the work feels more like a charitable offering than engagement in a vocation. There's a risk that the work will be done superficially, for the one who is working is engaged only temporarily, either to meet an external expectation or to soothe an uneasy conscience.

Writing in the 1930s, at a time of great wealth disparity in our country, John Dewey noticed many substantial gestures of charity and philanthropy occurring in the society. Dewey acknowledged these gestures as expressions of "good will and altruism," but he also "partly" saw them as "the manifestation of an uneasy conscience." He observed that such acts of generosity "testify to a realization that a regime of industry carried on for private gain does not satisfy the full human nature of even those who profit by it."[4]

In other words, systems only designed to make money don't necessarily make us feel whole. Dewey noted that the acts of charity affirm an impulse toward "social responsibility which the system as a system denies."[5] We can reflect on community service in this same light. A curriculum that is not oriented to solving real-world problems and grappling with deep and mature questions of engaged citizenship can leave us feeling incomplete. And so we seek completeness in other gestures of citizenship—often as afterthoughts, in the after-school hours.

Instead, our core curriculum should have a citizenship focus, through and through. The best service we can render our communities is a program of study that engages all of our young people in exploring and even trying to solve some of the important citizenship challenges our society is facing. This relates to the notion that curriculum relevance should derive from the deeply felt needs of individuals and the community.

The director of career and workforce development at Randolph Union High School, in central Vermont, has developed several courses that are called "deployed classrooms," designed to correlate with the needs of the broader citizenry, individual students, and their families. The "deployed classrooms" are largely oriented toward the world of work outside the school, exposing students to professionals in various fields and engaging students in the wielding of adult tools to complete adult tasks.

The deployed classrooms are populated like courses, with groups of students; these are not individualized internships. In a time when individualization and personalization too often connote solitary work—isolated students facing computer screens—it is important that schools continue to place primacy on the classroom community as an entity that has value for the collective learning and reflection that happens in the company of peers. Here's how two of this school's deployed classrooms are described in the school's course catalog:

- *Entrepreneurship and Manufacturing:* How does manufacturing fit into the fabric of Vermont, and how has technology changed the manufacturing workplace? How can any person with a great idea for a product turn that idea into a solid business? Students will develop in-depth answers to these questions as they pursue this Community Based Learning (CBL) offering at the GW Plastics plant in Royalton, VT. From a request for a quote (when a company asks the manufacturer to build them a product), to designing the molds on a CAD system and then building them, to purchasing the necessary raw materials, to scheduling, programming, and employing the state-of-the-art machines and robots, to making the product (and ensuring each piece passes a quality test), right to finding the best way to ship off the finished product, students will learn firsthand the capacities, challenges, and rewards of entrepreneurship and manufacturing.
- *Water Management: Public Policy & Practicality:* One of Vermont's greatest resources is its water: you can't depend on your Mountain State to remain Green unless you understand how to manage water and keep your supply of it healthy. Water is a natural, vital, and incredibly powerful force. It is necessary to maintain life, but it is also capable of astounding destruction. Its forms of destruction come slowly, quietly seeping or rushing madly and wildly. From drinking water wells to storm water to the water that floats our boats, water seeps into nearly every aspect of civic life, and it impacts nearly every career. In this course, we will explore a variety of careers, and the law, theory, thinking, practicality, and discipline that figures into dealing with water. This course is intended to provide a model for developing a local talent pool for occupations that make use of civil engineering and community planning skillsets. Further, the knowledge gained will benefit those who tend toward fields relating to construction, natural resources, water quality, and general contracting.[6]

On the continuum of curriculum that gets to work, on the one extreme we have ivory tower abstraction, on the other we have curriculum that hits the street and engages young people in local life, culture, and economy. These two deployed classrooms exist on the latter end of the continuum. The water management class, for instance, includes more than thirty off-site visits to professionals in various fields, and fewer than twenty in-classroom days a semester. That's a lot of excursions to organize, a lot of scheduling and coordination. The manufacturing class is much more site-specific and only successful because of a deep relationship formed between the school and the local manufacturer—professionals teaching each other, over time, learning how to speak each other's language and how to meet each other's needs.

These classes are possible largely because the school has chosen to invest in special resources, human resources, like a director of workforce development. This role comes with special capacity to model and support curriculum development that gets to work through community partnerships designed to meet the economic and citizenship needs of the community. However, once developed and up and running, these classes, with all of their school-community partnerships and relationships, can be handed off to traditional classroom teachers. Once the model has been refined and improved, and new institutional routines and relationships have taken hold, such classes become easier for a teacher to take on, and they can serve as models for what is possible on a smaller scale: a unit or project within a particular class.

Local manufacturers and other employers in rural zones see a population that is aging, with many young people choosing to leave the state. And yet these employers desire an educated and home-grown workforce: high school and college graduates who will join their teams for the long haul, learning a trade or profession, returning the employer's investment in their professional development through hard work, diligence, and dedication. Courses like the deployed classrooms are designed with the needs of the citizenry in mind. They are based in notions of local service or charity—but their potential for serving the community is extensive and deep.

2. From Guest to Partner

The educators and other professionals involved in implementing the deployed classrooms described above rarely refer to each other as guests. They are partners, interconnected and interdependent. A "guest speaker" can come and go, with little expectation for depth of relationship and little interest in the lasting consequences of the visit. The guest is not a resident, and the work has less meaning to them because they do not live with the results. Better we seek partners than guests. Partnerships endure, and partners care about the work the other is doing in the short and long term.

Teachers and schools can establish many different types of partnerships with professionals in the community: as instructors who engage directly with students in their learning, as assessors and evaluators of student work, and as advisors to particular programs or courses. Because citizens bring with them the needs and desires of the community outside the school, forging such partnerships inherently helps bridge the abstraction-application gap.

Instructional partners are community members who join the teacher in exposing students to expertise in a particular domain. The Project-Based Learning (PBL) Lab at Randolph Union High School makes this a standard practice. In a youth media course called Radio Free Randolph, the teacher collaborates regularly with a producer at a local radio station. She helps the teacher in instructing the students, provides feedback on works in progress, and helps students polish pieces that she eventually airs at the station where she works. In another elective called the Racial Justice Alliance, teachers partner with a local youth development organization to bring experienced facilitators to hold complex and challenging conversations in the course, and to help train the youth to lead such conversations with others in the community.

The PBL director supports teachers in designing these courses, and this person gathers wider support for the PBL Lab by annually gathering a group of advisors to consult on PBL offerings and provide feedback on student work at the end of each year. It's not always easy to get these citizens to the school many times in a given year, but an advisory board need convene only once or twice a year, and this is a good way to engage leaders of various sectors— CEOs, presidents, directors, business owners, and others—who can contribute their insights to big-picture strategic thinking, and who can hold the school informally but powerfully accountable for teaching and learning that gets to work.

All of a school's talk of career readiness risks being no more than lip service if the school doesn't involve professionals from related careers in the assessment of student work. Who better to help judge a student's emerging expertise than a professional in the field? Of course, the certified teacher is the one who ultimately has to say whether a student has met the school's standards, but assessment feedback can and should come from people other than teachers, people whose careers connect to the discipline.

Some schools create formal forums for citizens to participate in the evaluation of student work, such as panels that evaluate summative projects or papers. The work of schools in the New York Performance Assessment Consortium is a prime example. Semester and year-end performance tasks in various academic domains are presented and defended before panels of teachers and outside evaluators, using common rubrics. It takes time and staffing resources to execute well, but it is worth the effort. The citizens involved get an authentic glimpse of the work of the school, and they leave with a sense that their expertise is of value to the children and educators in their community.

3. From Fieldtrip to Fieldwork

At the end of their school year, students in a PBL elective at Randolph Union were asked to make a presentation of learning to their advisory board. The course was called Archeology and Indigenous Peoples: What Can the Buried Past Teach Us about the Present? The board included several important evaluators, including a funder whose organization provided the class a grant to travel to an archeological dig in Arizona in the fall; teachers from the school; and a local homeowner who has a farm in the hills of a neighboring town. This homeowner had offered her property to the students as a site for their spring work: a local archeological dig in and around the colonial-era foundations of a barn that had fallen and disappeared long ago. The students spent many days on her property over the course of the spring semester, a fieldwork site that allowed them to—literally and figuratively—dig deep into the learning.

A field*trip* can be like tourism. There's a visit, a passing through, and a return home. Much can be learned, but typically students do little during the trip to transform the environment and see the impact of their labor. They work very little on or in the field. Field*work*, however, has a different connotation: people labor at the location, working in or with the human or natural environment. There is a better chance of developing competence in the skills required for the work, and motivation to become competent at the task.

King Middle School, an Expeditionary Learning (EL) school in Portland, Maine, for many years has been a model for educators seeking examples of how to meld classwork with fieldwork. For instance, one of the school's 2013 "learning expeditions" involved fieldwork studying invasive species. The unit of study, undertaken by a division of the school called Windsor 7, was titled Alien Invaders:

> The students and teachers of Windsor 7 are joining forces with the City of Portland, and the Gulf of Maine Scientific Research Institute to address Maine's invasive species epidemic. Along the way, we will be collecting data on invasive species in Maine. As scientists, we will work to study invasives at Biddeford pool and to reduce an invasive plant in Portland. We will be creating impact studies and will present our findings to local decision makers. [7]

Place-based environmental education is a logical way for educators to integrate fieldwork into courses that get to work. Another EL school, in Colorado, engaged students in a 2015 study of local waterways. The work was anchored in an English class, which opened with the reading of a book about people exploring the Grand Canyon's Colorado River. The description of the expedition includes mention of several fieldwork sites:

> By the end of the semester in May, five sections—about 130 students—in teacher Ryan Montgomery's sophomore English class will have learned water hydraulics on a classroom water table, visited the hydroelectric plant at Tacoma on the Animas River north of Durango, rafted on the Animas River and spent three days at Glen Canyon Dam, Antelope Canyon and the Powell Museum in Page, Arizona.[8]

Spending three days at a fieldwork site allows for depth of learning and real-world skill development and application. When planning curriculum, teachers and those who support them should consider taking students to places that can be visited more than once, where students can get to know the hosts and the environment, and have opportunities to work collaboratively on projects in those locations.

4. From Audience to Consumer

The students at the archeological dig performed work that was meaningful to them and to the woman whose property they were exploring. They were doing work she wanted to have done. In this way, she was like a consumer, a client. We might also call her an *authentic audience*, a term educators often use when discussing student work that culminates in a demonstration of learning to people who care. But a few terms from the lexicon of the market economy better connote the kind of relationship that exists when students do work that inherently has the needs of other people in mind.

When students are working with and for a consumer, customer, client, or beneficiary, they are working with and for some of the most authentic audiences there can be. Such an audience will do more than passively watch and applaud; the audience observes and inspects with the eyes of those who intend to employ the product of the labor. This motivates the child to do a good job and wield tools with competence.

Technical education or vocational education programs often do work for clients or consumers: constructing a building, cooking food for events or for purchase, repairing an automobile. A career and technical center understands that students of all types are hungry for opportunities to employ knowledge as it functions in adult occupations. With diversifying its student body in mind, the leadership at the Randolph Technical and Career Center (the Tech Center) in Vermont has diversified program offerings in recent years such that the heterogeneity of the student body now challenges the stereotypical notion that vocational education is for blue-collar fields only. There is a strong film program, a strong graphic arts program, and a pre-pre-med nursing program. These programs and others draw students who, in a traditional high school classroom, might otherwise not have many opportunities for applied learning. There's much that traditional high schools and their educators can learn from our vocational centers.

One year, students from both the Tech Center and the PBL classes at the traditional high school jointly partnered with a local community development corporation to support the organization's annual meeting. The high school was asked by the director of the corporation if the school could host the event. The administration said yes—as long as there were ways to get students involved. The corporation was more than willing to involve students. From the Tech Center, students in Culinary Arts prepared and served food, students in Graphic Arts helped design program materials, students in Business Management collaborated on the agenda and staffed the registration tables and, as part of the content of the evening, students from the Digital Film program shared documentary films.

Participants affirmed seeing the sense of pride and competence in the students, and students saw the fruits of their labors enrich the evening and please their clients. In addition, the experience challenged many community members' conceptions of what high school and vocational education can be. After the film presentations, for instance, there were many questions for the Tech Center students from the attendees. One of the questions, from a woman whose face was full of wonder, was simply how these students felt being at the Tech Center. Between the lines, she was asking, "How does it feel for kids like you to be in that building with the kind of kids who study auto mechanics, diesel engines, forestry, and building trades?" The film students responded, matter-of-factly, that there's nothing but goodwill, mutual respect, and the shared understanding that everyone is just doing their thing, working on something that matters.

Students from the regular high school then proceeded to challenge the common assumptions of what a high school curriculum entails. Some of the students present were taking courses in the PBL Lab, tackling a tangible problem in the community, state, or world—and doing so in collaboration with local partners. At the time, one of these classes was focused on income inequality. The work these students shared at the community event was in fact a proposal to partner with the community development organization itself: to help them educate local citizens on the availability of underutilized low-interest loans. The students had studied micro-lending as a means of poverty reduction, and had already met with the executive director of this local corporation. Now they were ready to take the collaboration to a new level. This same group of students had also been to the state capitol, working with one of the state representatives to design legislation proposing a new levy on capital gains to support higher education grants to low-income students. This was the students' idea.

One community member wrote to school leaders after the evening gathering: "I am so glad that I came to the meeting at the school tonight. Seeing the enthusiasm of the staff, hearing the students, and seeing their projects continues to inspire me." Another community member sent this note: "I think it is safe to say that each and every person there was impressed with the caliber of the faculty and students in their craft and their characters. For myself, I could not have been more proud or impressed if they were my own kids up there." It's meaningful that this note includes mention of "craft," for this is essential: that students are skilled in a craft, competently wielding adult tools to complete adult tasks.

Adults in the community need not be the only clients, recipients, consumers of services provided by students. An elective focused on Restorative Justice, mentioned above, ultimately led to the students providing services to the school. "Do our schools and courts treat people fairly?" was the essential question. At the start of the year, students engaged in explorations of criminal justice and the school-to-prison pipeline, which led to an inquiry into six years of discipline data from their own school and work on focus groups with students who had experienced getting into trouble.

By mid-year the students had made presentations to faculty and had been trained in restorative justice circles and peer mediation, and finally they had begun their own facilitation of mediations and post-suspension re-entry circles. Discussions that had once only been led by a principal, counselor, or faculty member were now being led by students. Adults were important mentors in how to use the tools—discussion and mediation protocols—but by the end of the year, young people were doing much of the work, providing an important service to the school community.

"I CAN DO"

Young people are hungry to speak their identities through their labors. They will do this no matter what. The question, again, is what materials do we give them on which and with which to labor?

When the Restorative Justice class reviewed trends in their school's discipline data, they noticed a sharp decline in incidents after tenth grade. The class speculated that after that grade, some of the students who didn't fully feel a sense of place in the normal high school classrooms—which aren't that different from normal middle school classrooms in previous years—move on to eleventh-grade programs at the Tech Center, where they feel more valued and competent. These are not the only students who enroll in the Tech Center programs, but some of them certainly are boys and girls who once punched walls, cursed at teachers, or felt more quietly disengaged. At the Tech Center many are engaged in more productive expressions of force and voice. They get into a lot less trouble in school.

It is worth the investment in resources that help traditional core academic disciplines bridge the abstraction-application gap. Schools do well to reallocate staffing resources to make these investments because teachers need extra support to put students to work in partnership with the broader community.

The core academic disciplines—math, science, social studies, and English—require this extra support to bridge the abstraction-application gap because pedagogies of applied learning are not inherent in how we traditionally train teachers to teach. In other subject areas, it is much more integral to the traditions of the discipline that students are using their skills in ways that they are used in the adult world. In the arts, especially, and in after-school pursuits like athletics, students use adult instruments and tools, and perform before audiences that care. In the arts and in athletics, kids are engaged in activities that closely parallel how adults and professionals demonstrate their skills in those same domains. The tools are the same. The demonstrations of learning are, as in the adult world, performances, contests, exhibitions, and the sense of competence that comes with using adult tools to perform adult tasks. These are amplified through public demonstrations of learning.

When it comes to authentic demonstrations of emerging competence—that antidote to painful adolescent feelings of inferiority—the core academic disciplines could learn a lot from traditions in the arts, from other traditional offerings like drivers' education, and of course from career and technical education. Fieldtrips should become fieldwork. Passive audiences should become engaged consumers of student work. Occasional guests should become regular partners in teaching and learning, helping our young people develop competence and find their place, answering "who am I?" with "I can do."

QUESTIONS FOR REFLECTION AND DISCUSSION

1. In this chapter, we note that driving cars and hunting with guns are two commonplace invitations to young people to wield powerful adult tools for heavy practical tasks. This can inspire us to see what is possible in other domains. What heavy practical tasks need doing in your community—that students could be invited to approach through the school curriculum?

2. In what ways do the schools you know bridge the abstraction-application gap? What is working well? What could be done more effectively? How?

3. In your own life, have you ever answered the question "who am I . . .?" with "I can do . . ."? What work, tools, and skillsets constitute important aspects of your sense of self?

4. Do any of the four priorities for the Get to Work classroom seem appropriate to your school context? Why or why not? What benefits might there be? What concerns?

Chapter Eight

GET META

The hearts of most sixteen-year-olds are made of finer stuff. They do not want to be adolescents. They want to be young men and women.

—Garret Keizer[1]

Our young people know that there are problems to be solved in their world. To not be invited to solve them does injustice to their capacities and brings frustration, apathy, and anger—all of which can lead to harm, both to individuals and to the wider community.

The aggression inherent in adolescence isn't evil needing a victim—it's a drive needing productive outlet. This is why Jeremiah swaggers and brags of beating down the meat-flesh of his victims in the street. We've given him no other substance to impact, shape, or deconstruct. This is why the girls draw their own blood. They need to produce and see something that has meaning corresponding to their pain. This is why Roberto contemplates the bullet, and why other boys plot to kill their peers, knowing it means their own death. They'd rather contemplate the certainty of being dead than being nobody.

What our young people are seeking is identity coherence. In a violent and unjust world they can gain identity coherence through acts of violence and injustice, or they can gain it through more peaceful means. They can lash out with fists and knives and guns, or they can wield different tools to creatively attack the injustice that their hearts know needs undoing.

One such tool is language itself—and language about the self. Self-reflection and meta-cognition are pathways to seeing and identifying the self. These skills are gained, as with any skill, through practice. And knowing oneself and expressing that knowledge happens largely in and through language.

The companion imperative to empowering students to feel and act in powerful ways is the necessity of helping them voice why they feel and act the way they do.

Garret Keizer, an eloquent writer and veteran teacher, reflected in the 1980s on "the recent invention of adolescence." His characterization of adolescence as an invention was certainly informed by the popular explosion of Hollywood films made for and about teenagers in the 1980s. Keizer is not impressed by these and other popular portrayals of youth. The students this teacher knows, from rural and small-town New England, need something from their world other than affirmations of pettiness and prurience. They need their world to challenge them "to purposeful leadership," to "provoke them to creative rebellion," to "acquaint them with great ideas."[2] Keizer comes to this conclusion:

> [T]he recent invention called adolescence appeals to them about as much as it appeals to me—not much at all. Puberty is beautiful; adolescence can be as cheap and trashy as the interests that prey upon it. As an idea, it is far more appealing to ten-year-olds who want to talk "dirty" and to certain thirty-five-year-olds who want to live the way ten-year-olds talk. The hearts of most sixteen-year-olds are made of finer stuff. They do not want to be adolescents. They want to be young men and women. They believe in a promised land. And if we are not inclined to believe in something like the same thing, our every effort to help them amounts to a betrayal.[3]

Keizer is affirming the importance of a curriculum that is personal, that is political, and that compels young people to do work that the world needs doing. He's also raising our awareness about the kind of mirrors our society offers young people. Into what glass do we ask them to look? In what ways do we help them reflect upon who they are? What aspects of themselves do we help them to know better?

"I think, therefore I am" is not enough. It doesn't nearly capture what it means to be a human being. "I think about thinking, therefore I am" comes closer to it, and closer to what adolescents especially need. Research on student achievement has been conclusive on this. Cultivating self-reflection and meta-cognition are among the teaching strategies with the highest leverage in raising student achievement. This is evident to any effective teacher, and it's evident in meta-analyses of student achievement studies from across the globe, like those of education researcher John Hattie.[4]

Thinking about thinking has an impact on achievement because it helps instill a growth mind-set in young people who may otherwise have accepted a certain fixed definition of who they are and what their brains can do. It's not hard to understand why a young person might be inclined to settle into a fixed intellectual identity, even a negative one, at a time of so much physical change and identity flux. Adolescents will seek, as we all do, certainty in times of change.

And so adults who work with young people are confronted with a paradox: we want them to feel, through their ideals and actions, that they know who they are with some certainty and fixedness—but we don't want them to feel like they are finished becoming who they are.

Teachers must hold a growth mind-set and cultivate the same in kids. We must convey to them: You're not finished—and this is as true of your brain as it is of your heart. Your heart may feel pain, but it doesn't have to feel it so badly, so fully, and in such solitude. Your hands may feel ready for little other than wringing, but there is much they can do, and powerfully. Your gut may feel twisted—with guilt, sadness, doubt, rage—but we can help you name the feeling, know its source, and help you feel less troubled.

OPEN AND HONEST REFLECTION

Educators and parents know what the guarded, un-reflective, un-self-aware young person can sound like. After a fight, for instance, some students will say they can't remember what they did or why. "I just black out when I get mad," a student might say. Sometimes the child whose grades are low will say at a conference, "I'm just lazy," or "I just need to try harder." These students can't or don't want to talk about what's really going on. They don't want to discuss skills they've not yet gained, relationships that distract them, or perhaps a disability, or problems at home, or deeper emotions that trouble underneath. They want to end the conversation with statements like "I just don't get it," or "I'm just not a math person," or "I hate reading," or "I don't know," or silence. They don't yet feel safe or skilled at being vulnerable and self-reflective.

To help young people reflect openly and honestly, they need modeling and chances to practice thinking and talking about *why* they do what they do. In every corner of the school, adults can offer young people tools for reflection that help them think about thinking and feeling. And it is important to not compartmentalize this work. Cultivating self-knowledge is not just the responsibility of the guidance faculty or counselors. Each teacher and each curriculum has a role to play. Four priorities inform our work in the Get Meta classroom:

1. Think out loud; state the obvious
2. Name expectations and reflect on progress
3. Assess by sitting with
4. Study adolescence with adolescents

GET META: FOUR PRIORITIES

1. Think Out Loud; State the Obvious

Teachers can model and encourage students' awareness of themselves in the world simply by stating the obvious and thinking out loud. What do we notice in students? What do we notice in ourselves? What are we doing now? What are we going to do? Talking tactfully and appropriately about what we are noticing and feeling is one way to get meta.

There's no special technology. Indeed, thinking out loud and stating the obvious are practices intuitive to most parents of infants and toddlers. Imagine a mother holding an infant in her arms or looking down at the baby lying on a blanket. The mother's face appears over the face of the baby and the baby smiles. The mother says, "Yes, I see you smiling. What a big beautiful smile!" The mother smiles too.

Or perhaps the baby frowns or cries. The mother may frown too, and ask what's wrong. Or she may wonder aloud, "Are you hungry? Do we have to change your diaper?" Or she may know what's wrong and state the obvious, "Yes, we need to change your diaper." Or "Yes, I know you're getting too warm in this blanket."

For the young child, several things are happening here. As we discussed earlier, there is an "I see you" acknowledgment of the child's existence that is happening when the caregiver reciprocates and mirrors. Trust in the responsiveness of the world is being established and affirmed. Security and secure attachment are being built. In addition, the caregiver is providing language for feelings. The adult is naming emotions and sensations. Over time, these word-names will become part of the child's lexicon, circulating in thought and spoken in voice.

Eventually, the words the adult has given will help the child articulate and thereby better control the emotions and sensations that are being experienced. The toddler, for instance, who is angry at what has been offered for dinner and is preparing to throw the food on the floor might instead name the emotion and postpone the act: "I don't want this! I want to throw on the floor!" This postponement of immediate action, as Dewey would say, allows the child to delay the disruptive act, decide against it, or it permits the child to allow adults the time to intervene and assert their authority, redirecting the anger and averting the crisis.

In her book *The Magic Years*, Selma Fraiberg, a professor of child psychoanalysis, wrote about the special power of language:

> [T]he uniquely human achievements of control of body urges, delay, postpone-
> ment and even renunciation of gratification are very largely due to the higher
> mental processes that are made possible by language. The human possibility of
> consciously inhibiting an action and renouncing, if only temporarily, an ex-

pected satisfaction, is largely dependent upon the human faculties of judgment and reasoning, functions which are inconceivable without language.[5]

Language continues to function in much the same way in adolescence as in the younger years. Simply by thinking out loud and stating the obvious, educators can likewise model and offer the power of language to help adolescents better name and master their feelings and sensations.

Guidance along these lines is common in recent school reforms that come under the heading of "trauma-informed" practice. And, as Alex Shevrin Venet notes in her article, "8 Ways to Support Students Who Experience Trauma," these strategies are effective with all students: "As with many strategies to support a sub-group of students, these strategies can positively support most students with or without a history of trauma."[6]

One pair of strategies Shevrin Venet stresses is creating predictable routines and easing transitions between elements of the day or the lesson. For students with trauma in their backgrounds, this is especially important for major sensory transitions, such as introducing noise, turning off lights, and fire drills. But it is also important with predictable transitions, and simply talking out loud about what the class is doing and going to do is effective: "Give time warnings ahead of activity transitions (three minutes until we switch groups . . .)." But what if the transition doesn't go well? What if you are feeling frustrated as a teacher? Shevrin Venet advocates transparency, thinking and speaking out loud:

> During a class in which I'm feeling overwhelmed, instead of trying to hide that, I can use it as a learning opportunity by naming it and modeling a coping strategy. "Hey everyone, I'm feeling pretty flustered because that last activity didn't go how I thought it would. When I'm feeling flustered, it helps me to stretch for a minute. Let's all shake it out together."[7]

When teachers do this, it shows students that it's appropriate to notice and name their own emotions. Modeling and teaching positive coping skills benefits all students by normalizing the fact that we all have tough emotions sometimes and need to use strategies to manage them. As Shevrin Venet notes, the guidance here is "very simple."[8] But it may not come naturally to educators who feel the need to always present to students a face of total control. But this thinking and talking out loud, as long as adequate composure is maintained, works. Explaining to students how you feel models the intellectual apprehending of an emotional state. You can also model self-control and meta-cognition by telling students how you feel now and how you are likely to feel if certain events or behaviors continue.

Imagine the teacher who perceives too little focus on the task at hand and prepares to warn students about what will happen if the lack of focus continues. The warning can come in a form that again models emotional awareness and self-control: "I am reminding you in a calm voice right now, but if we aren't able to get back on task, you're going to notice my tone of voice change because I am losing patience and I want you to hear that." This conveys to the students that they are in the presence of an adult who has self-control and it models how emotions can be discussed and directed toward specific goals.

Another strategy of Shevrin Venet's trauma-informed teacher tool kit is telling the students what you see in them. This is a way to honor the trauma-informed axiom, "connect before correct," and it is another mode of mirroring and refusing to present a still face. If a student seems frustrated, upset, sleepy, or agitated, we can name what is noticed as a first step to helping the student step outside their emotional state, see themselves and how their body is behaving, and potentially make more informed choices about how to manage those emotions. Co-regulation is another term we could use to describe such interactions, which again are common in the parenting that takes place in a child's early years.

Imagine the student who walks into class and puts her head down. The teacher approaches her and before "correcting" and asking her to sit up and attend to class, the teacher says, "I see you have your head down on the desk." A question can follow, "Are you feeling tired? Hungry?" This stating of the obvious can go a surprisingly long way to honoring the reality of the student in the moment, and helping the student understand their own bodies and feelings so that they can better manage them.

Thinking out loud and stating the obvious—about one's self and one's students—may seem more appropriate for young children than adolescents. But we must remember that the pace of change of an adolescent's body is so accelerated in this phase of life, it is almost like they are becoming new people who need to see and know themselves anew. Meta-cognitive adults, who model how to use language to know and manage emotions, will help cultivate the same traits in students as they explore and discover who they are newly becoming in their adolescent years.

2. Name Expectations and Reflect on Progress

As with our emotions and thoughts, teachers in the Get Meta classroom will clearly name the goals of the endeavor, both the academic standards to be reached as well as the habits and dispositions that students may need in order to reach those academic goals. When written well and explicitly integrated into teaching and assessment, stating the standards for which students are asked to develop proficiency can help students better understand what they are doing, and why. Reflecting on the self in relation to the standards will also help illuminate areas of strength and areas for further growth.

Across the country, standards-based teaching and assessment is a reform leading to significant changes in how educators articulate goals to students and monitor progress. Depending on the state in which the reforms are taking place, standards-based instructional practices may go by other names, such as competency-based, proficiency-based, and mastery-based. These reforms have in common the principle of considering academic goals separately from the habits of work that may help students reach those goals. Being good at multiplying fractions and being on time to the class where a student learns how to multiply fractions are two different skill sets. The one skill is a mathematical one; the other has to do with punctuality, a transferrable skill that applies across domains, which some schools classify as a "Habit of Work." Schools may also have "Habits of Mind" or "Habits of Heart," outlining for students what critical-thinking skills and interpersonal traits are valued in the school.

One student may be good at reading, but struggle with organization and punctuality. Another student may be good at reading, but struggle with collaboration in groups. A third student may be a punctual, well-organized, and respectful collaborator, but struggle with reading comprehension. Each of these students deserves assessment feedback from adults that helps them meta-cognitively understand their various strengths and needs, which is the first step in figuring out how to meet those needs.

3. Assess by Sitting With

Deborah Meier, an educator who has founded—and inspired the founding of—many successful schools, likes to remind her colleagues and others that the origin of the word assessment is in the Latin root *assidere*, "to sit with." Meier is reminding us of the need to pause, slow down, and talk. Sitting with a child in patient dialogue helps the student develop self-understanding, learn how to frame goals, and see how to organize energies toward the fulfillment of those goals.

The Mission Hill School in Boston, founded by Meier and others, has produced a video series to share their practice. In "A Year at Mission Hill—Chapter 9: Seeing the Learning," we see students preparing for the culminating eighth-grade portfolio defense. The narrator informs the viewer: "Standardized tests are administered at Mission Hill, but teachers here find that direct contact and conversation are the most accurate way to judge if a child has mastered a skill or concept—or to figure out a new strategy to help them on the path toward greater understanding."[9]

Throughout the video we see images of teachers sitting with and talking to students: math teachers, English teachers, science teachers, interacting with students at computers, students with pieces of writing, students producing works of art. By the end of the video we see children sitting with or standing before groups of adults who take interest in their learning and work. In each setting the essential process is the same: be with the child, listen, probe for understanding, and reflect out loud with him or her on what is solid and what needs improvement.

Randolph Union Middle School in central Vermont, has an eighth-grade portfolio defense as well, modeled in part on what is done at Mission Hill. A short note from the school administration explains to the middle school students what belongs in their portfolio:

> Dear RU Middle School Students,
> Your portfolio is a place to gather artifacts of your personal learning journey at RU. It has two components: a Google Site, where you put work from your Google Drive folders, and a binder, where you organize paper copies of your work. Many of the artifacts that you select for this portfolio will come with teacher feedback, rubrics/grades, and your own self-reflections attached.
>
> At the end of Middle School, you will participate in a Portfolio Defense, a conference at which you show that you understand yourself as a learner and that you are ready to make the passage into high school. In addition to being an important rite of passage, the Portfolio Defense is an important step in preparing for future moments when you will be asked to reflect, write, and speak publicly about who you are—your values, interests, strengths, and areas for further growth. This happens when seeking employment, when applying to college, and as part of Senior Project. We look forward to working with you on your personal learning journey these next few years!

The portfolio's table of contents outlines five separate required sections:

1. *My Life: Past & Present:* In this part of your portfolio, you will collect artifacts that relate to your upbringing, your life outside of school, your values and beliefs.
2. *My Community: Strengths & Challenges:* This part of your portfolio includes artifacts that relate to what you are learning about the challenges and strengths of our local community and broader society. It should also include artifacts that reveal what you can do and are doing to make our community and world a better place.
3. *Content Knowledge:* Artifacts in this section should show academic strengths, progress you have made, as well as challenges and areas for future growth. Your classroom teachers—through rubrics and learning intentions—will help you understand which standards connect to the different assignments, projects, and assessments.
4. *Habits of Heart & Habits of Work:* Artifacts in this section should show strengths, progress you have made in these habits, as well as challenges and areas for future growth. Your classroom teachers— through rubrics and learning intentions—will help you understand

which standards connect to the different assignments, projects, and assessments.

5. *My Future: Goals, Plans & Dreams:* Artifacts in this section connect to your short-term, mid-range, and long-term goals—and evidence of progress toward those goals. In addition to your advisor and teachers, our School Counselors, Senior Project Director, and Director of Career & Workforce Pathways will help you have experiences that produce artifacts for this section.

"Senior Project" was mentioned twice in this table of contents. Senior Project is a capstone graduation project that likewise embodies the modality of assessment as *sitting with*. Students must have a mentor that they work closely with in the community for a certain number of hours as they complete their personalized project. They must meet with a panel several times over the course of the year as part of progress monitoring, and at the end of the year they must present their work in person to the panel in another kind of defense.

In addition, between eighth grade and senior year, students at this school engage in a tenth-grade portfolio defense, another reflection on their last two years of progress. And every year there are two conferences with families that are to a large degree student-led, with support from the student's advisory teacher. By the time senior year comes around, students are well practiced at sitting with their teachers and other adults to discuss their work. They thereby come to know themselves well.

4. Study Adolescence with Adolescents

The structures noted above, which allow adults to sit with students to reflect with them on their goals and progress, are largely structures that exist outside the individual classroom. Inside the classroom, conferencing with students is a possibility that depends for its depth and effectiveness on class size, pacing requirements, and other factors. So we will return here to a fourth approach to getting meta-cognitive with adolescents that can be integrated into almost any curriculum and classroom: the study of adolescence with adolescents.

The psychiatrist Stuart Twemlow asserts, "Children should know about adolescence. They should be taught about identify diffusion." He goes further, suggesting that young people should know about "premature identity foreclosure" and how "the adolescent is very prone to influence by peers, much more so than they are in an adult life," and how there are dangerous capacities in adolescence, such as the psychology and the capacity "to form cult-like groups that propose a continuation of prejudicial, omnipotent, and delusionally fixed ideas."[10] How to do this? A psychology course is one avenue, and many schools have such courses. But other disciplines also have a place here, in both how and what is taught.

It is essential to have pedagogies across the school that ask students to reflect on their work, self-assess their efforts, show their thought processes, and revise and integrate feedback. It is also important that young people encounter curriculum content that enables adolescent self-reflection and self-understanding. We can do this with mirrors and lenses: curriculum content can mirror young lives and experiences, and young lives and experiences can be lenses through which to understand curriculum content.

Science classes, for instance, can integrate teaching and learning about the child's own body and brain development—the adolescent brain and body in particular. Biology, anatomy, and physical education classes can help young people better understand why they move, do, and feel what they are doing and feeling. Social studies classes can bring to the forefront those themes of human history that are particularly relevant to adolescence: status hierarchies in human societies, the bully/bystander/victim dynamic in case studies of oppression and war, the identity journeys—family histories and teenage years—of women and men who leave their mark on history. English classes can develop their reading lists by keeping in mind the same kinds of themes and lenses. If students are reading *Moby Dick*, why not use the language of adolescent development and social dynamics to discuss the story: Is Ahab a bully or a victim-avenger? Where does his homicidal-suicidal rage originate? What kind of bystanders are Ishmael and the crew? Which of their own fears and insecurities do they ask this doomed whale and their doomed captain to embody? Teaching content through such themes can help us to help young people better self-reflect and ultimately self-regulate.

SELF-CONTROL

Cultivating self-regulation and self-control are important goals of the Get Meta classroom, and it is worth pausing to consider how self-control is related to self-understanding and to identity coherence. Some readers might appropriately wonder: If our goal for young people is a coherent, positive, and powerful sense of self, might not an emphasis on self-control limit self-discovery, which can come through creative and unconstrained exploration of one's world and one's powers to shape it?

Indeed, adolescence is a time of experimentation and the challenging of norms and expectations. Impulsivity and a lack of restraint are inherent in adolescence and will lead to new understandings of self. But ultimately we want our young adults to be able to make intentional choices. Impulse and intuition have their place—especially empathic intuition toward others—but so does the deliberate, intentional application of energies toward a goal. We want our young adults to make thoughtful decisions grounded in an honest understanding of their needs and capacities, as well as the needs of the world around them.

John Dewey went as far as to say that "the ideal aim of education is the creation of the power of self-control."[11] Adolescence is a tumult of impulse, a time when the prefrontal cortex is still developing. And so, as Dewey came to see long before the insights of neuroscience, "the crucial educational problem is that of procuring the postponement of immediate action upon desire until observation and judgment have intervened."[12] Think before you act. Be master-of, not mastered-by, your impulses. This is, ultimately, about what we might call freedom.

"Freedom resides," says Dewey, "in the operations of intelligent observation and judgment," and teachers who take an active role in providing language and concepts to help students understand why and how we are doing what we're doing are "an aid to freedom, not a restriction upon it."[13] Being free is very much about being able to know one's drives, motivations, abilities, habits, and purpose—then to pass judgment and act. Our young people know freedom when they take deliberate action and make informed choices based on knowledge of their world and who they are in it. Without this capacity, they are much more likely to simply obey and blindly follow.

And despite their capacity for rebellion, adolescents can blindly follow very well. They can follow adult instructions, follow unhealthy family habits, follow outdated cultural traditions, follow the directions of dangerous peer pressures—and worse, follow the blood-will-out demands of rage. Before concluding this chapter, let us return to the potentially violent rage of adolescence.

A CHILD POSSESSED

Danvers, Massachusetts, is Old Salem. It is the town located adjacent to the seaside village called Salem. It is the once-agrarian lowland where the colonial era witch trials took place, where people executed other people, mostly women, because they were believed to be possessed by demons.

On one side of town is the Homestead of Rebecca Nurse, a woman convicted of witchcraft and executed in 1692. Across town, the backyard of a stately colonial home fallen into disrepair was discovered to have been a site where a girl named Tituba once lived, a girl herself accused of occult practices, who sent Old Salem into turmoil with her assertions that the devil was among them. In Tituba's case, and in other witch trials, it was often a young person, possessed or tormented by some kind of spirit, who precipitated the hunt for a sorcerer or some other tangible embodiment of the cause of the child's affliction.

The idea that a young person could be possessed by demons was not an uncommon notion at the time, nor is it unfamiliar to many cultures across the world today. Such beliefs serve various functions, including helping to explain the sometimes confounding disturbances that can characterize childhood, especially preverbal childhood: early deaths, mysterious illnesses, erratic and irrational behavior. To see the devil's hand at work, possessing the child, may help adults explain what seems cruel, unfair, and otherwise unexplainable in the behavior of kids or the workings of fate upon children.

In this same town of Danvers, 350 years after the witch trials, what explanation do we have for what possessed the high school boy who murdered his young female math teacher? In 2013, what demon?

For confidentiality reasons, a scarcity of details trails such incidents when the accused is a minor. We can read online that he is of mixed race, his father African American; that he moved a lot and had recently moved to Massachusetts from Tennessee, where his family was enduring a difficult divorce. The details of what he did to his teacher, Colleen Ritzer, are easier to find: "Chism," one can read in the Boston Globe, "who was 14 at the time of the attack, allegedly followed Ritzer into a bathroom at the school shortly before 3 p.m., slashed her throat, partially stripped her, and stole her cell phone, credit cards, and two driver's licenses. He then allegedly took her body, in a recycling bin, to a wooded area behind the school, authorities have said. Chism allegedly raped Ritzer twice . . . "[14]

Who is this boy? What was his schooling like? Is this a case where a different school experience in his younger adolescent and pre-adolescent years could have shaped his identity differently? Is it even fair to ask? And more questions: What if this young African American boy who sexually assaulted and killed his white female teacher had read Richard Wright's *Native Son* in school? Had he? In the right learning environment, could exploring the complex themes of such a novel have helped him differently apprehend his own experience and differently execute his fate?

Native Son has a plot driven by the murder and dismemberment of a white woman by a young black man. What if Phillip Chism had read this? What if he'd also read James Baldwin's letter to his fifteen-year-old nephew, in which Baldwin tells the boy that the world into which he was born intends to destroy him—and then tells him that love is the only way out.

It may not have mattered; for this boy has probably demonstrated that he's among that less-than-1-percent of the population that experts like Stuart Twemlow say we should remove from the normal school setting. And Philip Chism perhaps hadn't been in any school long enough for any of the educators' observations or intuitions to tell them this. So it may not be fair to speculate that his choices might have been otherwise had he encountered some carefully taught classes that reflected back to him his deep rage and questions.

But we have to believe that expressions of violence can be prevented, and even if these speculations about curriculum reform and adolescent identity development aren't fair to apply to this case, it doesn't mean that this incident can't affirm the dangers of adolescent rage and the importance of schooling that reflects and humanizes the emotional lives our children are living.

Whether a child is at, or near, or never approaching the violent act, the job of the educator is to know the child and help them know themselves. The child can make better choices this way—like Melville's Ishmael, who took himself to sea. Ishmael knew himself well enough to control the darker impulse and walk instead toward the harbor, where he found important work, camaraderie, adventure, and even hope in the face of extreme destruction.

QUESTIONS FOR REFLECTION AND DISCUSSION

1. In what ways do the schools you know ask students to reflect on their work, show their thought processes, revise, and integrate feedback?
2. What do you think of John Dewey's assertion that "the ideal aim of education is the creation of the power of self-control"?
3. In what ways do the schools you know help young people know themselves?
4. Do any of the four guidelines for the Get Meta classroom seem appropriate to your school context? Why or why not? What benefits might there be? What concerns?

Conclusion

In an age of upheaval and tumult, educators mustn't minimize the potential that violence holds as a means to know one's self and feel a sense of power, agency, and identity. The white supremacists and antifa (anti-fascist) bands that have clashed in our country's streets in recent years affirm that violence can shape the world and the bodies of others in ways that furnish a vivid sense of impact, agency, and identity. You can see your impact in clear relief when you bloody the face of another.

An affirmation of the power of violence to provide identity coherence is not an endorsement of the path, but an indication of how crucial it is to illuminate alternative paths. And the alternate paths can be just as powerful. Many writers and leaders have illuminated this dichotomy. The memoir, *Narrative of the Life of Frederick Douglass, an American Slave, Written by Himself*, is particularly illuminating in this regard, for Douglass is a man who has experienced the identity-affirming and liberating power of both violent and nonviolent expression

Douglass's story contains two particularly vital and contrasting turning points in the evolution of his identity. The first might be called "regeneration through violence."[1] Douglass has been an enslaved man. He is subject to the terrific violence that slavery perpetrates on the body of the subjected. At one point, an overseer, Covey, approaches him for yet another routine crushing of his body and spirit. But Douglass fought back: "at this moment—from whence came the spirit I don't know—I resolved to fight; and, suiting my action to the resolution, I seized Covey hard by the throat; and, as I did so, I rose."[2]

From whence came this spirit of resistance? Franz Fanon, Algerian philosopher and scholar of colonial oppression, might say that it is the spirit of a historical self being reborn, forcefully reshaping specific circumstances of space and time. This rebirth is a violent one: a redirection of the violence that has historically ordered and defined the life of the oppressed:

> The violence which has ruled over the ordering of the colonial world, which has ceaselessly drummed the rhythm for the destruction of native social forms and broken up without reserve the systems of reference of the economy, the customs of dress and external life, that same violence will be claimed and taken over by the native at the moment when, deciding to embody history in his own person, he surges into the forbidden quarters. [3]

In resisting his overseer, Fredrick Douglass enters forbidden quarters. His fingers digging into the neck of Covey, he enters the white body and draws out the blood. They grapple for a long time, and Douglass is never beaten. It kindles a sense of himself as a man:

> This battle with Mr. Covey was the turning point in my career as a slave. It rekindled the few expiring embers of freedom, and revived within me a sense of my own manhood. . . . It was a glorious resurrection, from the tomb of slavery, to the heaven of freedom. My long-crushed spirit rose, cowardice departed, bold defiance took its place. [4]

Give me identity or give me death. In a world of violence, Douglass affirms the power of physical force to achieve personhood, confidence, triumph. As Fanon writes, "At the level of the individual, violence is a cleansing force. It frees the native from his inferiority complex and from his despair and inaction; it makes him fearless and restores his self-respect." [5]

Violent responses to a violent environment are very real options for young people in our world today. Our youth do not enter into riot, terrorism, suicide, and homicide on any kind of whim or as some trivial excursion. The violent acts they commit are the expressions of spirits seeking some kind of triumph over the denigrating forces that would keep those spirits down.

But there is another path toward achieving a coherent and dignified sense of self, one that Frederick Douglass's story likewise affirms. Of similar great importance in his journey is his mastery of literacy. He learned to read and write. Acquiring these skills happened before the moment of violent resistance to Covey. He was taught to read in early adolescence, and though his book learning was soon prohibited, he pursued his skill development and intellectual awakening subversively.

He discovered one particular book that he read at "every opportunity," a book that contained a dialogue between master and slave, in which the slave refutes every argument offered in favor of enslavement: "In this dialogue, the whole argument in behalf of slavery was brought forward by the master, all of which was disposed of by the slave." [6] Douglass discovered other texts that correlate to his struggles and strivings, helping him find words for the thoughts and feelings he was carrying inside:

> I read them over and over again with unabated interest. They gave tongue to interesting thoughts of my own soul, which had frequently flashed through my mind, and died away for want of utterance. . . . The reading of these documents enabled me to utter my thoughts. [7]

Douglass was, however, tormented by his new language and understanding: "It had given me a view of my wretched condition, without the remedy. It opened my eyes to the horrible pit, but to no ladder upon which to get out."[8] But Douglass lived with this torment, endured, survived. Later, after gaining his freedom, Douglas the abolitionist would wield the tools of literacy to tell his own story in powerful terms, working with others to trouble the master's house and bring slavery in this country to its end.

This story illustrates the identity-affirming might of both pen and sword. On the one hand, identity coherence and meaningful assertions of self can be achieved with force: violence can feel liberating and defining. But liberation and identity can also be achieved through words, the power of ideas, critical consciousness, and other tools. These seemingly tamer tools are the ones that teachers are trained to use, and train students to use. These tools only become powerful when we invite young people to wield them powerfully. Note how reading and writing for Douglass was never an exercise in mere abstraction or distraction. His skill development was anchored in deep relevance born of deep need, personal and societal. And the words he discovered on the page helped him discover himself in new terms: a meta-cognition that enabled him to fully see his place in a world troubled by injustices that he would work to dismantle.

Get Personal, Get Political, Get to Work, and Get Meta are imperatives that go hand in hand. When educators skillfully interweave these imperatives into the school lives of our children, we help them name the pains that reside in the world and inside themselves, and we give them tools to engage in struggle productively and peacefully. We reduce the likelihood that youth will choose violence as means to feel their power in a world that conspires against so many to make them feel powerless.

"WHO SAYS YES"

When graduation time came around, a student named Daren wrote a bunch of thank-you cards to the educators he'd come to know: his teachers, counselors, his principal. In the card he gave to his principal he thanked him for enabling the school to offer a course Daren took his senior year. This course was referenced in an earlier chapter, one of the Project-Based Learning

(PBL) electives offered at his school in central Vermont. As described by the teachers, the purpose of this course was to "respond to increasing community concerns about racial injustice in our local and national community." Part of their work would be to form a Racial Justice Alliance, "with the goal of raising awareness around racial injustice to create a safer environment for all community members."[9]

Daren identifies as biracial. In one of his college application essays he wrote about his long journey carrying the question, "Am I black or am I white?" He wrote about life growing up in Vermont:

> Moving to a town that is predominately white can be hard for a child that isn't white, or black, but biracial. The challenges faced by this, are somewhat different from what the Afro and white population face. Being told that you're not black, even though the DNA results say you are. Being told you're peanut butter, mocha latte, or caramel, because your skin isn't white. Throughout my life, I have been trying to develop a racial identity.[10]

The course Daren took his senior year proved a pivotal point in his struggle to name and speak his identity. This PBL course, which students could take for English or Social Studies credit, was one that followed the imperatives to Get Personal, Get Political, Get Meta, and Get to Work. The students were engaged at a deeply personal level in the essential questions of the class, which led them to historical analysis and reflections on contemporary society. Eventually they undertook an ambitious school-wide educational and activist campaign to raise the Black Lives Matter flag at the school, and they concluded the year by organizing and hosting the first statewide student-centered and student-run conference on the struggle for racial justice in Vermont schools. Hundreds of students and teachers from across the state attended.

Daren was a student—like many in the class—whose identity was shaped in powerful ways by the course. The students' energies, anger, questions, and convictions found channels in constructive directions. They were challenged and changed by the work of the class, as was the wider community.

At graduation time, in his card to his principal, Daren wrote, "The last six years have truly been a journey and I appreciate you helping me along the way." He shared gratitude for "valuable life lessons" and then, "I also want to thank you because the PBL course I was in actually helped me find a racial identity. I don't know who says yes to a course but I thank you."[11]

Indeed, both administrators and teachers have important roles to play in saying yes to courses like the one Daren took, in which teaching and learning is correlated to the needs of young people and the wider community. Youth today know trouble from a historically special host of sources: the stresses of intergenerational poverty, the sexism and racism of the dominant culture, the slow erosion of community by market forces, the easy brutality of online interactions, the sudden storms of a climate in turmoil, and the loss of loved ones to incarceration, addiction, and suicide. Schools can play a part in helping our young people transcend these troubles. There are ways to acknowledge the pains and questions our children carry, and to channel aggression in productive directions. But counseling, anti-bullying programs, and extracurricular activities are not enough. The key is to open up the very curriculum to the whole life of the child and the wider community.

Afterword

Every Lesson a Letter

What if teachers really mattered?

Most parents see their children for just a few hours on a school day; teachers are with them for six hours or more. What if those were the only hours in the day? Or what if children didn't have parents in their lives at all? Some don't. Imagine the child with no mother or father to teach her life lessons and mentor her in the deepest ways of the world. What if all that kids had were their schoolteachers?

Consider Denver, a girl in just such a situation. Her mother is debilitated by mental illness, no longer able to meet her own basic needs, much less support her daughter. Denver has lived a very sheltered life, and now in her late teens she walks the street, weakened and unsure. And then a woman named Lady Jones recognizes her. Jones is a teacher in the community and she had once taught Denver basic arithmetic and reading as a younger girl: "Other people said this child was simple, but Lady Jones never believed it."[1]

This is among the final episodes in Toni Morrison's novel, *Beloved*. The teacher beholds the child and sees "everybody's child" in her face, takes her by the hand, and pulls her close. The teacher learns that the girl and her mother are destitute, and so she connects the girl to the church community members who knew Denver as an infant, who knew her grandmother. They begin to provide food for Denver and her mother.

The teacher thus reconnects this girl to her community and to her past. Both the community and the child are both better for it. The adults rise to the occasion to care, and the child is nourished. And the teacher picks up where she left off years before, teaching the girl to read.

In this novel about personal and collective pain and redemption, this teacher is a redeemer. But there is another teacher in the story; he goes by the name Schoolteacher, and he is the narrative's primary symbol and instrument of injustice and cruelty. On the plantation where Denver's mother once lived, this man called Schoolteacher measures and studies: measures people's skulls and limbs, studies their phrases and ways. This educator's assessments and measurements confirm his bias, justify the violence, perpetuate the terror of the institution of slavery. The path from schoolhouse to master's house is short. Indeed, the spiritual architecture of these two houses seems very much the same.

Morrison's novel makes me wonder: Which of these teachers am I? Do my measurements of children simply confirm people's biases and perpetuate inequities? Does my sorting and ranking simply serve to buttress the brutal hierarchies of the wider society? I am troubled by the vision of Schoolteacher. I know that too many schools today do, indeed, sort and rank in ways that perpetuate oppressive and violent systems. I strive instead to be the teacher who sees my own child in the eyes of each child.

I want to be the educator who works with the community to nourish the child, to reconnect a child to her past, to fortify her for her future. And I want the community to learn and change, too, through these connections to the children. I hope the wider society will also change for the better through the work of young citizens who graduate into the world ready to dismantle injustice. Can I matter that much? Can I matter in that way?

NO SHELTERING

An inflated sense of self-importance doesn't serve anyone well. But in whatever we do, it's best to believe that we matter—and to try to matter in the right way. Believing that what we do shapes the world around us is really the only way to really feel responsible for what we do and for how our actions impact others. We must feel we matter and feel "responsible to life," as James Baldwin would say.[2]

So if teachers matter—and we do—then the curriculum we craft matters. Our syllabi, assessments, unit plans, and lessons must be written with deep caring for the children in our charge: a consciousness and curiosity about who they are in the world, a determined reckoning with how the world treats them, a faith in their capacity to change that world for the better.

When we believe we matter very much, then each lesson we write for the children attains the meaning of very personal communication, a personal letter written from our heart to the hearts and minds of children. Each lesson becomes a personal outpouring that we draft, perhaps tear up and then rewrite, appropriately troubled by how much to say and how to say it. We write our lessons in the spirit of the letter James Baldwin wrote to his fourteen-year-old nephew in 1963, and the letter Ta-Nehisi Coates wrote to his teenage son in 2015; the letter Jeremiah's girlfriend wrote to him in 2001, and the letters that Omar Saif Ghobash wrote to his seventeen-year-old son in 2017. Our curricula become letters like these.

In these letters there's no hesitation to engage in a frank accounting of injustice, no unwillingness to share insight as to why the child feels what he feels. Recall Baldwin's letter: "You were born into a society which spelled out with brutal clarity, and in as many ways as possible, that you were a worthless human being. You were not expected to aspire to excellence: you were expected to make peace with mediocrity."[3]

There is no sheltering the child. In Ta-Nehisi Coates's letter, he presents his son with cold, hard pragmatic warnings of upheavals yet to come, the legacy of racism, ceaseless consumption, and insatiable degradation of the natural world which yet continues today:

> The Earth is not our creation. It has no respect for us. It has no use for us. And its vengeance is not the fire in the cities but the fire in the sky. Something more fierce than Marcus Garvey is riding on the whirlwind. Something more awful than all our African ancestors is rising with the seas. The two phenomena are known to each other. It was the cotton that passed through our chained hands that inaugurated this age. It is the flight from us that sent them sprawling into the subdivided woods. And the methods of transport through these new subdivisions, across the sprawl, is the automobile, the noose around the neck of the earth.[4]

There is historical sense and contemporary context in these letters. There is an understanding of the allure of violence for many. Omar Saif Ghobash tells his son:

> The modern manifestation of the warrior is not the army general in his barracks with his loyal troops, or a young Napoleon, but rather the solitary, lonely, obedient, "misfit" type of young man who ends up being a suicide bomber or jihadist in Afghanistan or Syria. . . . The idea of the warrior is powerful.[5]

But alternative paths are also painted. Gobash wishes for his son: "Perhaps your generation can rethink its power in a positive way. Perhaps the modern Muslim warrior is one who embraces life in its complexity and fights for social and economic justice with his or her mind."[6] Yes, there are high hopes shared in these letters, and pride, praise, and reassurance. Consider all that Jeremiah's girlfriend stacks into this short paragraph to her boyfriend, a young man on the precipice of more violence and incarceration:

I really want to get you out of New York. I want you to see and experience new things. But please baby, just be patient. You know I'm gonna take care of you. I hope you're record label goes through. But I know it's gonna go through. I'm really proud of you.

There are other letters like these. Mothers write them too, of course. In *The Fire This Time*, a 2017 compilation of essays and poems born of contemporary African American life and struggle, the Haitian American writer, Edwidge Danticat, writes to her two daughters—or rather contemplates writing to them. She imagines telling them:

Dear Mira and Leila, I've put off writing this letter to you for as long as I can, but I don't think I can put it off any longer. Please know that there will be times when some people might be hostile or even violent to you for reasons that have nothing to do with your beauty, your humor, your grace, but only your race and the color of your skin. [7]

She confesses to her reader that this letter is yet ungiven to her girls. She wants to give them a letter that ends in hope. She tries to muster optimism and "look happily forward," but she cannot. [8] The world she sees cripples her optimism. Rather than strike a tone that she cannot own, she leaves it up to them to decide. She takes them on a journey to see a corner of the world that she needs them to know:

I took them to the border, the one between Haiti and the Dominican Republic, where hundreds of refuges were living, or rather existing. There they saw and helped comfort men, women, and children who look like them, but are stateless, babies with not even a bedsheet between them and a dirt floor. [9]

Danticat wants her daughters to know that these people are "our causes," reasons for compassion and action. She endeavors to "both tell and show them." [10] As a good teacher should, she strives to tell and show in balance.

As a parent and educator, I note the tone of these letters and reflections. I hear observations and questions, certainties and uncertainties delivered with equal urgency and force. There is no pandering to the whimsy of teenagehood, no unstructured invitation to indulge your interest, do your thing. There are instructions. There are clear warnings. Histories are told. There are lessons-I've-learned impartings. There are morals of the story. There are open questions of the gravest sort. There are efforts to reveal the world as it is, and to empower the children to formulate their own strong beliefs, to develop their competence to do important work in the only contexts that really matter: familial, personal, political, historical, moral, and ethical contexts where right and wrong, love and justice, peace and pain are on the line.

And the parent, uncle, mother, friend, mentor who is writing each letter knows full well that the child will chart his or her own path. They are not speaking forcefully in order to constrain the child. The child will take only what guidance resonates in the world he knows, and the child will embark from there. And though they know this, there is yet a duty that each of these adults refuses to abdicate: the duty to offer the armor, ideals, experiences, and questions that the adult has come to learn are necessary to survival and necessary to something more, called goodness. In this age of upheaval, young people need this kind of mentorship and teaching.

A NEW "WE"

The writers of the letters from which I draw inspiration here have black and brown skin, born themselves into a world in upheaval, and they are writing to their black and brown children who will know perhaps even greater upheavals still. Are white parents and teachers writing letters of this kind to their white sons and daughters?

I believe they are out there, but I have yet to come across them. Michael Eric Dyson's *Tears We Cannot Stop: A Sermon to White America* comes close. Dyson is black, however, and writes more to me, an adult. Dyson's prescriptions and instructions are guideposts that can guide me, as a white man, as a father, as a citizen. His "pedagogy of the problematic" is the kind to which I aspire, teaching that enables white students to "wrestle with the burdens and sorrows that honest talk of whiteness brings." Dyson is a teacher who wants his students—black, brown, and white—to "confront the brutal legacy of race with the kid gloves off, and yet respect each other's humanity."[11]

Our nation needs more white parents writing the letter to the white child about what it means to be a citizen of this country. Climate crisis is upon us. Our war-making in the Middle East and elsewhere continues unabated. On the inside, psychological depression is acute for many, and our efforts to kill that pain—and ourselves in the dark bargain—are increasingly effective. Our president is a man who, to borrow from Dyson, "whether he wishes to be or not . . . is the epitome, not only of white innocence and white privilege, but of white power, white rage, and yes, white supremacy."[12] Who is writing the letter to the white kids growing up in this country today?

Learning to Die in the Anthropocene, by Roy Scranton, also comes to mind. It's not a letter, but it's a meditation, an appeal to confront one's mortality, that grim whisper that whiteness is so good at silencing. Scranton isn't writing to a child, nor specifically to white people, but he's writing to a people who have behaved for centuries like children—spoiled children, consuming and self-serving, in immature denial of the destruction that they have foisted upon the world. ("Dreamers," Coates calls white people, because of a deep unwillingness to be awake to the daylight consequences of their deeds.[13] And Coates is right when he says a fierce wind is coming.)

Scranton's *Learning to Die* gets personal, offering confessional reflections about his time as a soldier in Iraq. And he makes it political, scientific, and historical too. And he demands his readers get to work. For Scranton, a crucial element of the work that needs doing is focused on identity. He demands we develop a new kind of humanism, a new way of understanding who we are:

> Within a few generations we will face average temperatures 7 degrees Fahrenheit warmer than they are today, rising seas at least three to ten feet higher, and worldwide shifts in crop belts, growing seasons, and population centers. . . . We face the imminent collapse of the agricultural, shipping, and energy networks upon which the global economy depends, a large-scale die off in the biosphere that's already well under way, and our own possible extinction as a species. If Homo sapiens survives the next millennium, it will be survival in a world unrecognizably different from the one we have known for the last 200,000 years.
>
> In order for us to adapt to this strange new world, we're going to need more than scientific reports and military policy. We're going to need new ideas. We're going to need new myths and new stories, a new conceptual understanding of reality, and a new relationship to the deep polyglot traditions of human culture that carbon-based capitalism has vitiated through commodification and assimilation. Over and against capitalism, we will need a new way of thinking our collective existence. We need a new vision of who "we" are.[14]

White teachers and parents need to do the work Scranton envisions: interrogating who we are, who we have been, and who we will be. But whether white or black or brown, the adults of this world all have a duty to help our children develop a powerful yet humble and compassionate vision of who we are in this troubled time. And teachers have a special duty, because we see the kids for six hours each day. Six hours a day. Even the parents who write these soul-searching-and-guiding letters typically don't get to spend six hours a day, five days a week, with their children. This frightening privilege falls to the teacher.

Notes

INTRODUCTION

1. James Hansen et al., "Ice Melt, Sea Level Rise and Superstorms: Evidence from Paleoclimate Data, Climate Modeling, and Modern Observations That 2°C Global Warming Could Be Dangerous," *Atmospheric Chemical Physics* 16 (2016): 3782, https://doi.org/10.5194/acp-16-3761-2016.

2. Anne Case and Angus Deaton, "Mortality and Morbidity in the 21st Century," *Brookings Papers on Economic Activity* (Spring 2017): 397–476, https://www.brookings.edu/wp-content/uploads/2017/08/casetextsp17bpea.pdf.

3. Rosa Cabrera (@TigeraC), "So much grief. We hurtin. There's a riot, asleep or awake, in all of us. We cope with injustice and trauma, until it becomes too heavy," Twitter, September 22, 2016, 1:41 p.m., https://twitter.com/TigeraC/status/779058089312092160.

1. CUT

1. Vermont Department of Health, "2015 Vermont Youth Risk Behavior Survey Report for Orange Southwest SU," 22, accessed April 19, 2019, http://www.healthvermont.gov/sites/default/files/OrangeSouthwest_SU.pdf.

2. Youth Communication, *My Secret Addiction: Teens Write about Cutting* (New York: Youth Communication, 2005), 11.

3. Youth Communication, *My Secret Addiction*, 24.

4. Mary T. Brady, "Cutting the Silence: Initial, Impulsive Self-Cutting in Adolescence," *Journal of Child Psychotherapy* 40, no. 3 (2014): 292, DOI:10.1080/0075417X.2014.965430.

5. Ernest Becker, *Denial of Death* (New York: The Free Press, 1973), 144.

6. Brady, "Cutting the Silence," 299.

7. Brady, "Cutting the Silence," 300.

8. Vermont Department of Health, "2015 Vermont Youth Risk Behavior Survey," 22.

9. Holly Hedegaard, Sally C. Curtin, and Margaret Warner, "Suicide Rates in the United States Continue to Increase," *NCHS Data Brief*, no. 39 (2018): 1, https://www.cdc.gov/nchs/data/databriefs/db309.pdf.

10. Vermont Department of Health, "2015 Vermont Youth Risk Behavior Survey," 22.

11. Anne Case and Angus Deaton, "Mortality and Morbidity in the 21st Century," *Brookings Papers on Economic Activity* (Spring 2017): 397.

12. Sabrina Tabernise, "Young Adolescents as Likely to Die from Suicide as Traffic Accidents," *New York Times*, November 4, 2016, https://www.nytimes.com/2016/11/04/health/suicide-adolescents-traffic-deaths.html.

13. Tabernise, "Young Adolescents."

2. SWAGGER

1. James Baldwin, *The Fire Next Time* (New York: Dell Publishing, 1964), 109.

2. Genesis 8:21.

3. Friedrich Nietzsche, *On the Advantage and Disadvantage of History for Life* (Indianapolis: Hacket Publishing, 1980), 11.

4. Nietzsche, *On the Advantage*, 63.

5. Mark Bowden, "Donald Trump Doesn't Want Me to Tell You This, But . . ." *Vanity Fair*, December 10, 2015, https://www.vanityfair.com/news/2015/12/donald-trump-mark-bowden-playboy-profile.

6. Marwan Bishara, "Small Hands Big Missiles: Trump's Dangerous Adolescence," *Al Jazeera*, January 9, 2017, https://www.aljazeera.com/indepth/opinion/2017/01/small-hands-big-missiles-trump-dangerous-adolescence-170109061803090.html.

7. Naomi Klein, "Daring to Dream in the Age of Trump," *The Nation*, July 3/10, 2017, https://www.thenation.com/article/daring-to-dream-in-the-age-of-trump/.

8. Erik Erikson, *Identity, Youth and Crisis* (New York: Norton, 1968), 29.

9. Erikson, *Identity, Youth and Crisis*, 29.

10. Erikson, *Identity, Youth and Crisis*, 28.

11. Cornel West, *Race Matters*, (New York: Vintage, 2001), 9–10.

12. West, *Race Matters*, 24.

13. Cornel West, *Democracy Matters* (New York: Penguin, 2004), 27.

14. West, *Race Matters*, 10.

15. West, *Race Matters*, 26.

16. West, *Democracy Matters*, 41.

17. West, *Democracy Matters*, 41.

18. Baldwin, *Fire Next Time*, 21.

19. James Baldwin, *The Price of the Ticket* (New York: St. Martin's Press, 1985), xx.

20. Baldwin, *Price of the Ticket*, xx.

21. Baldwin, *Price of the Ticket*, xix.

22. West, *Race Matters*, 10.

23. West, *Race Matters*, 29.

24. James Baldwin, *Fire Next Time*, 17.

3. STUMBLE

1. Roberto wrote: "Hollow point bullet—when fired air pressure is being built up at the center of the bullet. Doing this, the bullet expands making it wider in order to cause more destructive damage."

2. Roberto wrote: "Regular bullet (Full Metal Jacket)—The bullet is not carved out. Can create damage, but leaves exit wounds."

3. Ta-Nehisi Coates, *Between the World and Me* (New York: Spiegel & Grau, 2015), 22.

4. Bill McKibben, *Eaarth: Making a Life on a Tough New Planet* (New York: Times Books, 2010), 133 (emphasis in original).

5. David Owen, *Green Metropolis: Why Living Smaller, Living Closer, and Driving Less Are the Keys to Sustainability* (New York: Riverhead, 2009), 36.

6. Bill McKibben, *Deep Economy: The Wealth of Communities and the Durable Future* (New York: Holt, 2007), 95–96.

4. SEETHE

1. James Baldwin, *The Fire Next Time* (New York: Dell Publishing, 1964), 28.

2. Christian Picciolini, "Former Neo-Nazi: White Supremacy 'Is Certainly Not a Fringe Movement,'" interview by Michel Martin, *All Things Considered*, NPR, March 16, 2019, https://www.npr.org/2019/03/16/704137555/former-neo-nazi-white-supremacy-is-certainly-not-a-fringe-movement.

3. Ta-Nehisi Coates, *Between the World and Me* (New York: Spiegel & Grau, 2015), 61.

4. Omar Saif Ghobash, *Letters to a Young Muslim* (New York: Picador, 2016), 7.

5. Ghobash, *Letters*, 9.

6. Ghobash, *Letters*, 13.

7. Ghobash, *Letters*, 13–14.

8. Lawrence Friedman, "A Biographer's Reflections on a Decade-Long Process," in *The Future of Identity: Centennial Reflections on the Legacy of Erik Erikson*, ed. Kenneth Hoover (New York: Lexington Books, 2004), 38.

9. Ibid.

10. Erik Erikson, *Identity, Youth and Crisis* (New York: Norton, 1968), 72.

11. Erikson, *Identity, Youth and Crisis*, 176.

12. Herman Melville, *Moby Dick* (New York: Signet, 1980), 21.

13. Stuart Twemlow, "A Crucible for Murder: The Social Context of Violent Children and Adolescents," *Psychoanalytic Quarterly* 72, no. 3 (2003): 695.

14. Twemlow, "Crucible for Murder," 661.

15. Stuart Twemlow et al., "Assessing Adolescents Who Threaten Homicide in Schools," *American Journal of Psychoanalysis* 62, no. 3 (2002): 216.

16. Twemlow, "Crucible for Murder," 663.

17. Twemlow, "Crucible for Murder," 670.

18. Twemlow, "Crucible for Murder," 662.

19. Twemlow, "Crucible for Murder," 671.

20. Twemlow et al., "Assessing Adolescents," 223.

21. "School Violence Fact Sheet: 2016," Centers for Disease Control, accessed April 19, 2019, https://www.cdc.gov/violenceprevention/pdf/school_violence_fact_sheet-a.pdf.

22. Nel Noddings, "What Does It Mean to Educate the Whole Child?" *Educational Leadership* 63, no. 1 (September 2005): 8–13, http://www.ascd.org/publications/educational-leadership/sept05/vol63/num01/What-Does-It-Mean-to-Educate-the-Whole-Child¢.aspx.

23. *The Hungry Heart*, directed by Bess O'Brien (Barnet, VT: Kingdom County Productions, 2013). For more information, see thehungryheartmovie.org.

24. Twemlow et al., "Assessing Adolescents," 225.

25. Erik Erikson, *Identity and the Life Cycle* (New York: Norton, 1980), 98.

26. Ibid.

27. Stuart Twemlow, "A Crucible for Murder: The Social Context of Violent Children and Adolescents," *Psychoanalytic Quarterly* 72, no. 3 (2003): 665.

5. GET PERSONAL

1. Ann Marie Sacramone, "Civic Intersubjectivity" (paper presented at the American Psychoanalytic Association Annual Meeting, New York City, January 19, 2017).

2. Christopher Emdin, *For White Folks Who Teach in the Hood . . . and the Rest of Y'all Too* (Boston: Beacon, 2016),13.

3. Mary T. Brady, "Cutting the Silence: Initial, Impulsive Self-Cutting in Adolescence," *Journal of Child Psychotherapy* 40, no. 3 (2014): 293, DOI:10.1080/0075417X.2014.965430.

4. Sacramone, "Civic Intersubjectivity."

5. Ibid.

6. Kenneth Hardy and Tracey Laszloffy, *Teens Who Hurt: Clinical Interventions to Break the Cycle of Adolescent Violence* (New York: Guilford, 2005), 29.

7. Hardy and Laszloffy, *Teens Who Hurt*, 101.

8. Titus Kaphar, "Annette Gordon Reed and Titus Kaphar: Are We Actually Citizens Here?" interview by Krista Tippett, *On Being with Krista Tippett*, The On Being Project, June 29, 2017, https://onbeing.org/programs/annette-gordon-reed-and-titus-kaphar-are-we-actually-citizens-here-jun2017/#transcript.

6. GET POLITICAL

1. Carl Glickman, *Renewing America's Schools: A Guide for School-Based Action* (San Francisco: Jossey-Bass, 1993), 9.

2. Erik Erikson, *Identity, Youth and Crisis* (New York: Norton, 1968), 258.

3. Erikson, *Identity, Youth and Crisis*, 199.

4. Ibid.

5. Robert Frost, *Collected Poems of Robert Frost* (New York: Garden City Publishing, 1942), 323.

6. "Florida Student Emma Gonzalez to Lawmakers and Gun Advocates: 'We Call BS,'" CNN, February 17, 2018, https://www.cnn.com/2018/02/17/us/florida-student-emma-gonzalez-speech/index.html.

7. Emily Witt, "How the Survivors of Parkland Began the Never Again Movement," *New Yorker*, February 19, 2018, https://www.newyorker.com/news/news-desk/how-the-survivors-of-parkland-began-the-never-again-movement.

8. Jorge Rivas, "The Teacher Who Taught Students to Challenge the NRA on the Day They Lost 17 of Their Own," *Splinter News*, February 27, 2018, https://splinternews.com/the-teacher-who-taught-his-students-to-challenge-the-nr-1823355017.

9. Rivas, "Teacher Who Taught Students."

10. Martin Luther King, Jr., "The Other America," speech given at Grosse Pointe High School, March 14, 1968; recorded/transcribed by the Grosse Pointe Historical Society, Grosse Pointe, Michigan, https://www.gphistorical.org/mlk/mlkspeech/.

11. Randolph Union High School, "Personal Learning for the Common Good: A Conference for Teachers, Students, Community," promotional paragraph in State of Vermont Agency of Education "Weekly Field Memo" 10, no. 36 (October 5, 2016), https://education.vermont.gov/weekly-field-memo/volume-10-issue-36.

12. Personal email correspondence with the author, September 2, 2016.

13. Phillips Exeter Academy staff, "Courses of Instruction 2019–2020" (Course catalog, Exeter, NH: Phillips Exeter Academy, 2019), 19, 8, 61, 29, 24, https://www.exeter.edu/sites/default/files/documents/PEA-COI-2019-20.pdf.

14. Christine Olson, "Curriculum Catalog, Spring 2016," (Curriculum catalog, New York: the James Baldwin School, 2016), 7–8.

15. T. Elijah Hawkes, "Course Catalog, School Year 2017–2018" (Course catalog, Randolph, VT: Randolph Union High School, 2017), 12–13.

16. "Remarks by President Trump to the People of Poland," Krasinski Square, Warsaw, Poland, July 6, 2017, https://www.whitehouse.gov/briefings-statements/remarks-president-trump-people-poland/.

17. Jennifer Gonzalez, "The Big List of Class Discussion Strategies," *Cult of Pedagogy* (blog), October 15, 2015, https://www.cultofpedagogy.com/speaking-listening-techniques/.

18. Diana E. Hess and Paula McAvoy, *The Political Classroom: Evidence and Ethics in Democratic Education* (New York: Routledge, 2015), 4.

19. Hess and McAvoy, *Political Classroom*, 182.

20. Elizabeth Kleinrock and Heinemann Publishing, "Engaging Families as Partners in Equity Work," *Medium*, November 10, 2018, https://medium.com/@heinemann/engaging-families-as-partners-in-equity-work-780e420dc57e.

21. Ibid.

22. Hess and McAvoy, *Political Classroom*, 179.

23. Christopher Emdin, *For White Folks Who Teach in the Hood . . . and the Rest of Y'all Too* (Boston: Beacon, 2016), 143–44.

24. Emdin, *For White Folks*, 144.

7. GET TO WORK

1. John Dewey, *Democracy and Education: An Introduction to the Philosophy of Education* (New York: Macmillan, 1922), 268.

2. Katie Reilly, "Read Michelle Obama's Speech Condemning Donald Trump's Comments About Women," *Time*, October 13, 2016, http://time.com/4530580/michelle-obama-donald-trump-comments-sexual-assault/.

3. Erik Erikson, *Identity and the Life Cycle* (New York: Norton, 1980), 87.

4. John Dewey, *Individualism, Old and New* (New York: Prometheus Books, 1999), 44.

5. Ibid.

6. T. Elijah Hawkes, "Course Catalog, School Year 2017–2018," (Course catalog, Randolph, VT: Randolph Union High School, 2017), 30.

7. King Middle School, "W7 Past Expeditions" (King Middle School, Portland, ME), accessed April 19, 2019, https://king.portlandschools.org/expeditions/past_expeditions/w7_past_expeditions.

8. Alexis Margolin, "At Colorado's Durango High School, Students Explore Rivers from Many Angles," *EL Education* (blog), March 4, 2015, https://eleducation.org/news/colorados-durango-high-school-students-explore-rivers-many-angles.

8. GET META

1. Garret Keizer, *No Place But Here: A Teacher's Vocation in a Rural Community* (Lebanon, NH: University Press of New England, 1996), 16.

2. Keizer, *No Place But Here*, 16.

3. Ibid.

4. John Hattie, *Visible Learning: A Synthesis of Over 800 Meta Analyses Relating to Student Achievement* (New York: Routledge, 2009).

5. Selma Fraiberg, *The Magic Years* (New York: Charles Scribner's Sons, 1959), 115.

6. Alex Shevrin Venet, "8 Ways to Support Students Who Experience Trauma," *Edutopia*, September 14, 2014, https://www.edutopia.org/discussion/8-ways-support-students-who-experience-trauma.

7. Ibid.

8. Ibid.

9. "A Year at Mission Hill—Chapter 9: Seeing the Learning," directed by Tom and Amy Valens, video posted by ayearatmissionhill, May 23, 2013, https://www.youtube.com/watch?v=OfeBe2G7DDQ.

10. T. Elijah Hawkes and Stuart Twemlow, "Threat Level High (School): Curriculum Reform with Violence in Mind," *Schools: Studies in Education* 12, no. 2 (2015): 193.

11. John Dewey, *Experience and Education* (New York: Simon & Schuster, 1997), 64.

12. Dewey, *Experience and Education*, 69.

13. Dewey, *Experience and Education*, 71.

14. John R. Ellement, "Teen Accused in Teacher's Murder Investigated for Assault," *Boston Globe,* June 4, 2014, http://www.bostonglobe.com/metro/2014/06 /03/teen-accused-murder-danvers-high-school-teacher-being-investigated-for-assault-juvenile-detention-facility/ vN1yoCp7NrKtd5ENqm9KMP /story.html.

CONCLUSION

1. Richard Slotkin, *Regeneration through Violence: The Mythology of the American Frontier, 1600–1860* (Norman: University of Oklahoma Press, 2000).

2. Frederick Douglass, "Narrative of the Life of Frederick Douglass, an American Slave, Written by Himself," in *The Norton Anthology of African American Literature*, eds. Henry Louis Gates, Jr. and Nellie Y. McKay (New York: W.W. Norton & Company, Inc., 1997), 343.

3. Franz Fanon, *The Wretched of the Earth* (New York: Grove Weidenfeld, 1991), 40.

4. Douglass, "Narrative," 343.

5. Fanon, *Wretched of the Earth*, 94.

6. Douglass, "Narrative," 327.

7. Douglass, "Narrative," 328.

8. Ibid.

9. T. Elijah Hawkes, "Course Catalog, School Year 2017–2018" (course catalog, Randolph, VT: Randolph Union High School, 2017), 17.

10. Anonymous student, personal communication with the author, July 7, 2019.

11. Anonymous student, personal communication with the author, June 14, 2019.

AFTERWORD

1. Toni Morrison, *Beloved* (New York: Alfred A. Knopf, 1987), 247.

2. James Baldwin, *The Fire Next Time* (New York: Dell Publishing, 1964), 124.

3. Baldwin, *Fire Next Time*, 18.

4. Ta-Nehisi Coates, *Between the World and Me* (New York: Spiegel & Grau, 2015, 150–51.

5. Omar Saif Ghobash, *Letters to a Young Muslim* (New York: Picador, 2016),144–45.

6. Ghobash, *Letters*, 145.

7. Edwidge Danticat, "Message to My Daughters," in *The Fire This Time*, ed. Jesmyn Ward (New York: Scribner, 2016), 213.

8. Danticat, "Message," 214.

9. Ibid.

10. Ibid.

11. Michael Eric Dyson, *Tears We Cannot Stop: A Sermon to White America* (New York: St. Martin's Press, 2017), 99.

12. Dyson, *Tears We Cannot Stop*, 222.

13. Coates, *Between the World and Me*, 143.

14. Roy Scranton, *Learning to Die in the Anthropocene* (San Francisco: City Lights Publishing, 2016), 19.

Bibliography

Baldwin, James. "A Talk to Teachers." In *The Price of the Ticket*, 325–332. New York: St. Martin's Press, 1985.

Baldwin, James. *The Fire Next Time*. New York: Dell Publishing, 1964.

Baldwin, James. *The Price of the Ticket*. New York: St. Martin's Press, 1985.

Becker, Ernest. *Denial of Death*. New York: The Free Press, 1973.

Bishara, Marwan. "Small Hands Big Missiles: Trump's Dangerous Adolescence." *Al Jazeera*, January 9, 2017. https://www.aljazeera.com/indepth/opinion/2017/01/small-hands-big-missiles-trump-dangerous-adolescence-170109061803090.html.

Bowden, Mark. "Donald Trump Doesn't Want Me to Tell You This, But . . ." *Vanity Fair*, December 10, 2015. https://www.vanityfair.com/news/2015/12/donald-trump-mark-bowden-playboy-profile.

Brady, Mary T. "Cutting the Silence: Initial, Impulsive Self-Cutting in Adolescence." *Journal of Child Psychotherapy* 40, no. 3 (2014): 287–301. DOI: 10.1080/0075417X.2014.965430.

Cabrera, Rosa (@TigeraC). "So much grief. We hurtin. There's a riot, asleep or awake, in all of us. We cope with injustice and trauma, until it becomes too heavy." Twitter, September 22, 2016. https://twitter.com/TigeraC/status/779058089312092160.

Case, Anne, and Angus Deaton. "Mortality and Morbidity in the 21st Century." *Brookings Papers on Economic Activity*, Spring 2017, 397–476. https://www.brookings.edu/wp-content/uploads/2017/08/casetextsp17bpea.pdf.

Coates, Ta-Nehisi. *Between the World and Me*. New York: Spiegel & Grau, 2015.

Cohen, Joshua. "'Diseases of Despair' Contribute to Declining US Life Expectancy." *Forbes*, July 19, 2018. https://www.forbes.com/sites/joshuacohen/2018/07/19/diseases-of-despair-contribute-to-declining-u-s-life-expectancy/.

Cone, James. *The Cross and the Lynching Tree*. Maryknoll, NY: Orbis Books, 2013.

Danticat, Edwidge. "Message to My Daughters." In *The Fire This Time*, edited by Jesmyn Ward, 205–15. New York: Scribner, 2016.

Dewey, John. *Democracy and Education: An Introduction to the Philosophy of Education*. New York: Macmillan, 1922.

Dewey, John. *Experience and Education*. New York: Simon & Schuster, 1997.

Dewey, John. *Individualism, Old and New*. New York: Prometheus Books, 1999.

Douglass, Frederick. "Narrative of the Life of Frederick Douglass, an American Slave, Written by Himself." In *The Norton Anthology of African American Literature*, edited by Henry Louis Gates, Jr. and Nellie Y. McKay, 302–68. New York: W. W. Norton & Company, 1997.

Dyson, Michael Eric. *Tears We Cannot Stop: A Sermon to White America*. New York: St. Martin's Press, 2017.

Ellement, John R. "Teen Accused in Teacher's Murder Investigated for Assault." *Boston Globe*, June 4, 2014. https://www.bostonglobe.com/metro/2014/06/03/teen-accused-murder-danvers-high-school-teacher-being-investigated-for-assault-juvenile-detention-facility/vN1yoCp7NrKtd5ENqm9KMP/story.html.

Emdin, Christopher. *For White Folks Who Teach in the Hood . . . and the Rest of Y'all Too.* Boston: Beacon, 2016.

Erikson, Erik. *Identity and the Life Cycle*. New York: Norton, 1980.

Erikson, Erik. *Identity, Youth and Crisis*. New York: Norton, 1968.

Erikson, Erik. *Young Man Luther: A Study in Psychoanalysis and History*. New York: Norton, 1962.

Fanon, Franz. *The Wretched of the Earth*. New York: Grove Weidenfeld, 1991.

"Florida Student Emma Gonzalez to Lawmakers and Gun Advocates: 'We Call BS.'" CNN, February 17, 2018. https://www.cnn.com/2018/02/17/us/florida-student-emma-gonzalez-speech/index.html.

Fraiberg, Selma. *The Magic Years*. New York: Charles Scribner's Sons, 1959.

Friedman, Lawrence. "A Biographer's Reflections on a Decade-Long Process." In *The Future of Identity: Centennial Reflections on the Legacy of Erik Erikson*, edited by Kenneth Hoover, 23–42. New York: Lexington Books, 2004.

Frost, Robert. *Collected Poems of Robert Frost*. New York: Garden City Publishing, 1942.

Ghobash, Omar Saif. *Letters to a Young Muslim*. New York: Picador, 2016.

Glickman, Carl D. *Renewing America's Schools: A Guide for School-Based Action*. San Francisco: Jossey-Bass, 1993.

Gonzalez, Jennifer. "The Big List of Class Discussion Strategies." *Cult of Pedagogy* (blog),October 15, 2015. https://www.cultofpedagogy.com/speaking-listening-techniques/

Hansen, James. *Storms of My Grandchildren*. New York: Bloomsbury, 2009.

Hansen, J., M. Sato, P. Hearty, R. Ruedy, M. Kelley, V. Masson-Delmotte, G. Russell, G. Tselioudis, J. Cao, E. Rignot, I. Velicogna, B. Tormey, B. Donovan, E. Kandiano, K. von Schuckmann, P. Kharecha, A. N. Legrande, M. Bauer, and K.-W. Lo. "Ice Melt, Sea Level Rise and Superstorms: Evidence from Paleoclimate Data, Climate Modeling, and Modern Observations that 2°C Global Warming Could Be Dangerous." *Atmospheric Chemical Physics* 16 (2016): 3761–3812. https://doi.org/10.5194/acp-16-3761-2016.

Hardy, Kenneth V., and Tracey A. Laszloffy. *Teens Who Hurt: Clinical Interventions to Break the Cycle of Adolescent Violence*. New York: Guilford, 2005.

Hattie, John. *Visible Learning: A Synthesis of Over 800 Meta Analyses Relating to Student Achievement*. New York: Routledge, 2009.

Hawkes, T. Elijah. "Course Catalog, School Year 2017–2018." Course catalog. Randolph, VT: Randolph Union High School, 2017.

Hawkes, T. Elijah, and Stuart Twemlow. "Threat Level High (School): Curriculum Reform with Violence in Mind." *Schools: Studies in Education* 12, no. 2 (2015): 161–97.

Hedegaard, Holly, Sally C. Curtin, and Margaret Warner. "Suicide Rates in the United States Continue to Increase." *NCHS Data Brief* no. 39 (2018): 1–8. https://www.cdc.gov/nchs/data/databriefs/db309.pdf.

Hess, Diana E., and Paula McAvoy. *The Political Classroom: Evidence and Ethics in Democratic Education*. New York: Routledge, 2015.

Kaphar, Titus. "Annette Gordon Reed and Titus Kaphar: Are We Actually Citizens Here?" Interview by Krista Tippett. *On Being with Krista Tippett*, The On Being Project, June 29, 2017. https://onbeing.org/programs/annette-gordon-reed-and-titus-kaphar-are-we-actually-citizens-here-jun2017/#transcript

Keizer, Garret. *No Place But Here: A Teacher's Vocation in a Rural Community*. Lebanon, NH: University Press of New England, 1996.

King, Martin Luther, Jr. "The Other America." Speech given at Grosse Pointe High School, March 14, 1968. Recorded/transcribed by the Grosse Pointe Historical Society, Grosse Pointe, Michigan. https://www.gphistorical.org/mlk/mlkspeech/.

King Middle School. "W7 Past Expeditions." Portland, ME: King Middle School, accessed April 19, 2019. https://king.portlandschools.org/expeditions/past_expeditions/w7_past_expeditions.

Klein, Naomi. "Daring to Dream in the Age of Trump." *The Nation*, July 3/10, 2017. https://www.thenation.com/article/daring-to-dream-in-the-age-of-trump/.

Kleinrock, Elizabeth, and Heinemann Publishing. "Engaging Families as Partners in Equity Work." *Medium*, November 10, 2018. https://medium.com/@heinemann/engaging-families-as-partners-in-equity-work-780e420dc57e.

Margolin, Alexis. "At Colorado's Durango High School, Students Explore Rivers from Many Angles." *EL Education* (blog), March 4, 2015. https://eleducation.org/news/colorados-durango-high-school-students-explore-rivers-many-angles.

McKibben, Bill. *Deep Economy: The Wealth of Communities and the Durable Future*. New York: Holt, 2007.

McKibben, Bill. *Eaarth: Making a Life on a Tough New Planet*. New York: Times Books, 2010.

Melville, Herman. *Moby Dick*. New York: Signet, 1980.

Morrison, Toni. *Beloved*. New York: Alfred A. Knopf, 1987.

Nietzsche, Friedrich. *On the Advantage and Disadvantage of History for Life*. Indianapolis: Hacket Publishing, 1980.

Noddings, Nel. "What Does It Mean to Educate the Whole Child?" *Educational Leadership* 63, no. 1 (September 2005): 8–13. http://www.ascd.org/publications/educational-leadership/sept05/vol63/num01/What-Does-It-Mean-to-Educate-the-Whole-Child¢.aspx.

O'Brien, Bess, dir. *The Hungry Heart*. Barnet, VT: Kingdom County Productions, 2013.

Olson, Christine. "Curriculum Catalog, Spring 2016." Curriculum catalog. New York: The James Baldwin School, 2016.

Owen, David. *Green Metropolis: Why Living Smaller, Living Closer, and Driving Less Are the Keys to Sustainability*. New York: Riverhead, 2009.

Phillips Exeter Academy Staff. "Courses of Instruction 2019–2020." Course catalog. Exeter, NH: Phillips Exeter Academy, 2019. https://www.exeter.edu/sites/default/files/documents/PEA-COI-2019-20.pdf.

Picciolini, Christian. "Former Neo-Nazi: White Supremacy 'Is Certainly Not A Fringe Movement.'" Interview by Michel Martin. *All Things Considered*, NPR, March 16, 2019. https://www.npr.org/2019/03/16/704137555/former-neo-nazi-white-supremacy-is-certainly-not-a-fringe-movement.

Randolph Union High School. "Personal Learning for the Common Good: A Conference for Teachers, Students, Community." Promotional paragraph in State of Vermont Agency of Education "Weekly Field Memo" 10, no. 36 (October 5, 2016). https://education.vermont.gov/weekly-field-memo/volume-10-issue-36.

Reilly, Katie. "Read Michelle Obama's Speech Condemning Donald Trump's Comments About Women." *Time*, October 13, 2016. http://time.com/4530580/michelle-obama-donald-trump-comments-sexual-assault/.

"Remarks by President Trump to the People of Poland." Krasinski Square, Warsaw, Poland, July 6, 2017. https://www.whitehouse.gov/briefings-statements/remarks-president-trump-people-poland/.

Rivas, Jorge. "The Teacher Who Taught Students to Challenge the NRA on the Day They Lost 17 of Their Own." *Splinter News*, February 27, 2018. https://splinternews.com/the-teacher-who-taught-his-students-to-challenge-the-nr-1823355017.

Sacramone, Ann Marie. "Civic Intersubjectivity." Paper presented at the American Psychoanalytic Association Annual Meeting, New York City, January 19, 2017.

"School Violence Fact Sheet: 2016." Centers for Disease Control, accessed April 19, 2019. https://www.cdc.gov/violenceprevention/pdf/school_violence_fact_sheet-a.pdf.

Scranton, Roy. *Learning to Die in the Anthropocene*. San Francisco: City Lights Publishing, 2016.

Shevrin Venet, Alex. "8 Ways to Support Students Who Experience Trauma." *Edutopia*, September 14, 2014. https://www.edutopia.org/discussion/8-ways-support-students-who-experience-trauma.

Slotkin, Richard. *Regeneration through Violence: The Mythology of the American Frontier, 1600–1860*. Norman: University of Oklahoma Press, 2000.

Tabernise, Sabrina. "Young Adolescents as Likely to Die from Suicide as Traffic Accidents." *New York Times*, November 4, 2016. https://www.nytimes.com/2016/11/04/health/suicide-adolescents-traffic-deaths.html.

Twemlow, Stuart W. "Bullying Is Everywhere: Ten Universal Truths about Bullying as a Social Process in Schools and Communities." *Psychoanalytic Inquiry* 33, no. 2 (March 2013): 73–89. https://doi.org/10.1080/07351690.2013.759484.

Twemlow, Stuart W. "The Columbine Tragedy Ten Years Later: Psychoanalytic Reminiscences and Reflections." *Journal of the American Psychoanalytic Association* 60, no. 1 (2012): 1–10.

Twemlow, Stuart W. "A Crucible for Murder: The Social Context of Violent Children and Adolescents." *Psychoanalytic Quarterly* 72, no. 3 (2003): 659–98.

Twemlow, Stuart W., and Tanya Bennett. "Psychic Plasticity, Resilience and Reactions to Media Violence: What Is the Right Question?" *American Behavioral Scientist* 51, no. 8 (2008): 1155–83.

Twemlow, Stuart W., Peter Fonagy, Frank C. Sacco, and Eric Vernberg. "Assessing Adolescents Who Threaten Homicide in Schools," *American Journal of Psychoanalysis* 62, no. 3 (2002): 213–35.

Twemlow, Stuart W., Peter Fonagy, Frank C. Sacco, Eric Vernberg, and Jennifer M. Malcolm. "Reducing Violence and Prejudice in a Jamaican All Age School Using Attachment and Mentalization Theory," *Psychoanalytic Psychology* 28, no. 4 (2011): 497–511.

Twemlow, Stuart W., and George H. Hough. "The Cult Leader as an Agent of a Psychotic Fantasy of Masochistic Group Death in the 'Revolutionary Suicide' in Jonestown," *Psychoanalysis and Psychotherapy* 24, no. 4 (2008): 222–39.

Twemlow, Stuart W., Frank C. Sacco, and Stephen W. Twemlow. *Creating a Peaceful School Environment: A Training Manual for Elementary Schools*. Agawam, MA: T & S Publishing Group, 1999. http://www.backoffbully.com/PDF%20files/PeacefulSchools/manual.pdf.

Valens, Tom, and Amy Valens, dir. "A Year at Mission Hill—Chapter 9: Seeing the Learning." Video posted by ayearatmissionhill, May 23, 2013. https://www.youtube.com/watch?v=OfeBe2G7DDQ.

Vermont Department of Health. "2015 Vermont Youth Risk Behavior Survey Report for Orange Southwest SU," accessed April 19, 2019. http://www.healthvermont.gov/sites/default/files/OrangeSouthwest_SU.pdf.

Wallace-Wells, David. *The Uninhabitable Earth*. New York: Tim Duggan Books, 2019.

West, Cornel. *Democracy Matters*. New York: Penguin, 2004.

West, Cornel. *Race Matters*. New York: Vintage, 2001.

Whitman, Walt. *Leaves of Grass and Selected Prose*. New York: Rinehart, 1959.

Witt, Emily. "How the Survivors of Parkland Began the Never Again Movement." *New Yorker*, February 19, 2018. https://www.newyorker.com/news/news-desk/how-the-survivors-of-parkland-began-the-never-again-movement.

Youth Communication. *My Secret Addiction: Teens Write about Cutting*. New York: Youth Communication, 2005.

Recommended Resources

"A TALK TO TEACHERS" BY JAMES BALDWIN

All of the books and essays referenced in this book are significant to me. The relevance of many of them is discussed directly in the text, so I won't reiterate that here. James Baldwin is a writer referenced throughout this book. He has taught me as much about myself, and my country, as any other writer. I recommend his entire oeuvre of essays; one essay that I didn't explicitly reference in the book is Baldwin's "A Talk to Teachers." This piece—originally a speech delivered to educators—situates the work of classroom teaching in socio-political-personal-historical context. One can't read it and not reckon with how personal, political, and urgent our work is.

FACING HISTORY AND OURSELVES

The personal, political, and historical intertwine in the work of this organization. Their lessons and guidance are thoughtfully crafted for classroom teachers. Facing History and Ourselves helps us see how the hate and bigotry of today have historical roots, from which present problems derive and from which we can learn lessons to solve contemporary challenges. Off-the-shelf resources for teachers are offered on the organization's website (facinghistory.org), along with opportunities for deeper partnerships and professional development.

RETHINKING SCHOOLS

Here is a list of just a few Rethinking Schools book titles to entice you to check out the organization's resources: *Rethinking Mathematics*; *Teaching for Black Lives*; *Rethinking Bilingual Education*; *Reading, Writing, and Rising Up*; and *A People's Curriculum for the Earth*. Rethinking Schools (rethinkingschools.org) also publishes a monthly magazine featuring the work of educators whose classrooms Get Personal, Get Political, Get Meta, and Get to Work.

TEACHING TOLERANCE

The Teaching Tolerance website (tolerance.org) has a vast collection of resources. Teachers, try typing a topic you are teaching into the site's search engine and see what you get. I tried it with "algebra" and found a link to an article and lesson plan on school funding inequity. With lessons like these, the relevance of the subject gets connected to needs of the wider society. Teaching Tolerance is also a great site to find discussion norms and guidance on how to shape the discourse of the classroom so that it enables both kindness and courage.

YOUR LOCAL NEWSPAPER

Your curriculum will feel relevant to the identities of students and the community if the learning is contextualized in local needs and challenges. In addition to the national organizations and websites listed above, your local, regional, and state newspapers are a fine way to learn about challenges faced by the places our students live and the people outside the school who are working to address them.

ZINN EDUCATION PROJECT

Like Howard Zinn's book, *A People's History of the United States*, the resources offered by the Zinn Education Project (zinnedproject.org) emphasize the experiences of working people, people of color, women, and others whose stories are often untold in the traditional school curriculum. Teachers can search for resources by theme, time period, resource type—and the topics include all subject areas, from the arts to math, science, U.S. history, and global studies. If there's a story, for instance, in your local newspaper that you know connects to the lives of your students, a quick search of resources on the Zinn Education Project could help you connect the local topic to broader historical and contemporary contexts.

Index

About the Author

T. Elijah Hawkes has been a public school teacher and principal for more than two decades. He has worked in rural and urban school communities, including Randolph Union in central Vermont, and the James Baldwin School in New York City, where he was founding principal. His writings about adolescence, public schools, and democracy have appeared in various books, magazines, and online publications.

CPSIA information can be obtained
at www.ICGtesting.com
Printed in the USA
FSHW021252140820
72978FS